Crea

North West Regional Writers

Inquiries should be addressed to
Northwest Regional Writers
C/O Russ Hanson
2558 Evergreen Av, Cushing, WI 54006
Riverroadrambler @ gmail.com

FIRST EDITION
First Printing, December 2012

Inside this book you will discover a wide range of writing, composed of poetry, nonfiction, and fiction. In the fictional submissions, any resemblance to actual persons is purely coincidental.

Printed in the United States of America
at Createspace.com

All individual stories are under copyright of the authors who graciously gave permission for their work to be used in this anthology of stories written in the last five years by people who at one time or other have attended the Northwest Wisconsin Regional Writers meetings.

Table of Contents

4

5

Mission Statement

To foster excellence in writing through creative writing exercises, and assignment, conferences, workshops, contests, and retreats.

To critique one another's work in progress.

To encourage members to write creatively, diligently, and seriously.

To exchange ideas about writing, marketing, and life experiences.

To enjoy fellowship with other writers.

To welcome aspiring writers.

For more than 44 years the Northwest Regional Writers have been gathering together as an organization with this mission statement foremost in our minds.

"Creative Reflections" is the culmination of the last five years of our organizations joint writing experiences, and represents, in this anthology, a reflection of who we are and what we do. For those of us who have been members for an extensive period, as well as those who have recently joined, it has been and continues to be an enjoyable as well as a learning experience.

In this, our 6th book, we not only wish to share our creativity, but we also feel honored to be able to pay tribute by dedicating this book to three of our writers (Bernice Abrahamzon, (1921-2012) Maxine Fluegel, (1935-2010) and Doris Hanson (1928-2011). These gracious ladies who in their lifetime and, in their time with us, have enriched the lives of many, none the least of which are the fellow writers and members of our club. For those of us who have shared the writing experience with them we are indebted. It is our utmost desire to see in print, alongside of ours, the creative efforts they have shared with us. In this way we can better remember, and pass on to others, the magic of their words.

Denis Simonsen
For the Northwest Regional Writers

Bernice Abrahamzon

(January 21, 1921 - January 25, 2012) Bernice Vivian Abrahamzon passed into eternal life, January 25, 2012, at the age of 91 years and 4 days. Bernice was born January 21, 1921, at 1015 Madison Street, a home that the Kreitz family had built in Lake Geneva, Wisconsin. She was the daughter of Goldie Laura (Hovey) and Paul Dreitz, and was an only child.

Her father had been apprenticed to become a gardener. Bernice and parents lived on the Wacker estate, of Wacker Drive fame, and on the Zimmerman estate, Snug Harbor. Both of these estates were in suburban Chicago. His mentor was a man affectionately known as Uncle Bob McBride. In 1929 Bernice's father accepted a position as head gardener at the estates of Green Tree and Broadoaks near Oconomowoc, Wisconsin. Paul Kreitz worked there for 39 years.

Bernice attended Summit grade school, receiving an eighth graduation diploma, on real sheepskin. Bernice then attended and graduated from Oconomowoc High School in 1939. Bernice graduated from Milwaukee Downer College in 1943. Her college experiences and education was a life-long influence in her life. She also completed on semester of graduate work at Carrol College at Waukesha, Wisconsin.

At various times, besides caring for her ailing mother, Bernice worked for Carnation Milk Company, a local Sanatorium, and a Lonely Hearts company. She corresponded with her future husband Kenneth Lorn Abrahamzon for 3 years before they met. They were married March 4, 1945, at Oconomowoc, while Kenneth was still on active duty as a Marine Corps Aviator. They lived at Bunker Hill and Peru, Indiana, as WWII came to an end. Bernice and Kenneth returned to his home town of Superior, Wisconsin, so he could complete his college education. Kenneth accepted a teaching position at Ashland, Wisconsin. Bernice also taught there, teaching High School literature.

They moved to Sheboygan, Wisconsin, for one year, where Kenneth was technical director for Sheboygan Community Players, a professional theatre company. Bernice, Kenneth and boys moved to St. Paul, Minnesota, where Ken taught and directed plays at the Hihle Theatre on the campus of Macalester College. They lived on campus in facility barracks. They relocated to North St. Paul, Minnesota where Ken taught at North High for 15 years. In 1956 they moved to Lewis, just for the summer to be near Ken's parents who had retired there. They rented a small house for 30 dollars a month from Alice and Gust Saros.

In 1959 they bought a small farm, south of Lewis, and never moved again. Both Bernice and Ken became active in the Methodist Church in Lewis, which became life-long commitments. Eventually Bernice became employed by the Inter-County Leader, first the bindery, ending at age 72 as proof-reader. Bernice wrote the Lewis news for more than 30 years and the "Do You Remember" feature. She wrote a weekly column "Behind the Sign Post" for many, actually unknown number of years, it could be as many as forty.

Bernice authored three books, was a charter member of the North West Regional Writers club and Indianhead Gem and Mineral Society. In fact she was the last charter member of both those organizations. She wrote many, many articles and was published in several newspapers and journals. Bernice was preceded in death by her parents, infant brother, Kenneth, husband for 41 years, all of her aunts, uncles and cousins. In a way she was the last leaf on the tree.

She is survived by her three sons, Drew Eric, Timothy Kirk, Tod Marshall, friend Sheila Staples, who she considered a daughter or daughter-in-law, by some nieces and nephews, by members of clubs and organizations she belonged to, her church community, by friends and readers of her writing, most of whom she didn't know by name but loved never-the-less. We will mourn our loss at her passing and cherish her memory.

REMEMBERING BERNICE by Denis Simonsen

Flower Child

You might have been a flower child
One who worshiped nature
Digging in the musky soil
Breathing it into life

Your green thumb transforming
Brown to red, yellow, lavender and orange
Your innocent laughter luring
Friends into your garden

Gathering seeds of memory
Transplanting them with cursive script
Sowing them on fertile soil
In willing minds and hearts

Autumn has touched your cheek
In your eyes sharp apple cider twinkles

Transferred to the page
You sow and gently pass to us
The gifts that help us grow

A TRIBUTE TO BERNICE by Mary Jacobsen

Our Northwest Regional Writers' meetings are not the same without Bernice. Yet, the writing club that she and the late Ruth Bunker Christiansen founded in 1966 is not only still in existence, but is as strong and vital as ever. Bernice set us on the way and we continue to be inspired by her example and encouragement.

Writing was her passion and she kept reminding us that we're writers and, as writers, we should submit our writing to contests, newsletters, newspapers, magazines, and other writing outlets, an activity that Bernice continued almost to the end of her life. She reminded us that writers use all of life's experiences in their writing, and that nothing is lost on a writer.

How can we not thank her?

Bernice wrote with humor and good will. She sometimes poked gentle fun at changing customs or fashions but she never belittled people. An example appears in a column she wrote a few years ago about a hospital experience which she depicted as a play she called "Biopsy." She had a "walk-on role," and the protagonists were the surgeon and the anesthesiologist, with a supporting cast. She mentioned that she was never sure what to call a staff member—nurse, aide, technician, since everyone dressed so informally. When she'd been in the hospital before, she wondered why the cleaning lady was taking her pulse.

I hope Bernice knew how much we, the members of Northwest Regional Writers, appreciated all she meant to us, both as a club and as individuals.

And I hope our thanks hasn't come too late

BERNICE by Alice Ford

This beautiful lady came to Lewis with her natural curls and yellow eyes. Bernice always knew just the right words to day, always words to the wise. You couldn't see it, but we knew from day one, Bernice always wore a crown.

When she spoke the room would become so quiet. There wouldn't be a sound.

Her voice was like soft velveteen as she brought the sunshine in.

Bernice never gave up, she was there to win, she wanted you to win.

She pushed you, and loved you, and if you were down she pushed you back up.

Her soul was filled with Love and her heart was full. Bernice filled our cup.

TRIBUTE TO BERNICE by Mikhaila Lampert

Sunlight reached through the trees
Grasping like fingers at everything it reached
It painted shadows, this cool Spring morning,
Setting dips and valleys aglow in light.
She felt it warm her fingers; her
breath as she stood there
Admiring; jealous of its beauty.
Her feet whispered through the high grass,
casting shadows on her feet
She looked back to the wind,
watching her shadow dance and whirl.
Lying on her back, fog escaping above
Wet dew seeped into places unseen.
Golden buds; pink and yellow,
Called to her like a whistling fellow.
Feet back on the ground, pacing and
zigzagging, sunlight bathing the whole field.
She was exhilarated; alive. She loped by the
Sun, leaping and catching it.
Leaves fell upon her head, and she laughed.
The wind laughed too, and said, "You're oh so
beautiful...", as she danced into the arms of loved ones.

RARE GOLD by Kathyrn A Krantz

I've been missing my dear sweet lady friend. Missing her because of the many phone calls we shared together at night on the phone. I remember one birthday Jodi Pearson and I took Bernice out to lunch in Siren at the Pour House. If my memory serves me right Bernice had soup and I had chili. Bernice was always against buying coffee in the restaurants because it was too high priced. On the way into Siren she asked if we could stop at the drug store on the way home.

I had been listening to her conversations over the phone and I surmised that she had wanted some perfume. I am an Avon dealer and bought a perfume for her that is called Rare Gold. I explained in the birthday card that she was a rare breed and that God had refined her like gold so therefore she was rare gold in my eyes. On the way out of Siren I asked her if she had wanted to stop at the drug store and she said. "No, my friend, you gave me what I wanted there. I wanted perfume."

In one of her articles she said that her mother had made cake using coffee. I had the recipe and I sent it on to Bernice. I didn't know if she ever tried to make the cake from the recipe but I think she did get the recipe by mail.

On several occasions she tried to inspire me to write again. I would tell her "Bernice the words are all gone. I'm out of ideas." Again and again she would try to coax me to write but alas my words had all disappeared.

One other thing I do remember about Bernice was one of our telephone conversations and that went something like this:

"Kathy you must really try to find yourself a man. You know you're way too young to be a widow and living all alone out in the boondocks."

"Yes Bernice I am young but what about those three boys of yours? They aren't married are they?"

"No Kathy they aren't married but you'll never get them. They run like the wind when they think someone is after them."

"Well Bernice I'll bring my lasso and lasso one of them!"

"You'll have to lasso really fast because they run you know."

"Don't worry Bernice, I don't know how to lasso so I think they're pretty safe from me."

Lots of laughter came from both her and me at the end of that admission.

Yes, my friend is gone but not the love I have for her, for that is deep in my heart. The last time I saw Bernice she was in the nursing home and I held her hand and looked into her eyes and she said "You know I love you don't you?"

"Yes Bernice I do I love you too and that's what it's all about my dear sweet friend."
So perhaps as you read this, Rick, Timothy and Todd, may it gladden your hearts to know that your mom is not forgotten, she's just away from sight exploring new horizons of the universe. Perhaps there she will be classified as a rare breed and as rare gold.

Via Con Dios Amiga. Go with God, my female friend. Until we meet again I wish you well Bernice. All my love, Lady K.

Doris V. Hanson (1928-2011)

Doris passed away at her home in Trade Lake Township on August 11, 2011. This is the same house where she was born 82 years ago on November 26, 1928. She loved the country and especially the Trade Lake area. She was very proud of her Swedish heritage and she spoke Swedish fluently.

Doris attended Trade Lake #5 Elementary School and graduated from the Grantsburg High School in 1946. On September 20, 1947 she married George E. Hanson of Wood River Township. To this union four sons were born.

Doris worked as a mother, a farm wife, and later, a hospital cook at Burnett Regional Medical Center in Grantsburg. She loved painting, playing piano, writing and visiting with family and friends. She and her musical group, "The Get Togethers," spent many hours providing musical programs for area nursing homes and seniors groups. She always had time to help those less fortunate.

She is preceded in death by her parents, Victor and Elsie Swenson, her husband, George, and brothers, Gunnard and Einar Swanson. She is survived by her sons and daughters-in-law, Bruce and Mary Ann of New Richmond, Allen and Cindy of Centuria, Glenn and Susan of Clear Lake, and Thomas and Patti Jo of Grantsburg.

"Grandma Doris" as she was affectionately known, was especially proud of her nine grandchildren, Kathy, Laura, Erik, Jillian, Ryan, Jenni, Shari, Danny and Pierce and her 12 great-grandchildren.

GRAIN FIELDS by Doris Hanson

Methods of farming have changed over the last 75 to 100 years. What used to be a very slow process of tilling the soil with horse drawn machinery such as a one bottom plow while the farmer would walk behind, controlling the horse and lifting the plow then replacing it again into the sod and turning it over. Compare that now with today and the high powered tractors and a plow with so many shares and feet wide makes it almost unbelievable!

Not only was it a job to plow but the farmer had to also disk the field several times to break up the sod clumps then drag it so it was nice and smooth for seeding wheat, oats or barley. These grains were very important for the farmers to raise.

For example; wheat was used for making flour. There were three grindings of wheat. The first grinding took off the outside fiber hulls. This product was called bran. The second was the middling. The third and final grinding was flour that every homemaker needed for making bread and other baked goods. This grinding was all done at the grist mill. Almost every small town had a grist mill so farmers didn't need to drive a great distance to have their grain processed.

Oats and barley were used in their natural form for the chickens. It was called "scratch feed." They would take a few scoops and throw it on the ground outside in the summer or on the straw covered floor during the winter. It made the chickens excited and they would scratch quickly to find this food and gobble it up. It was also good exercise for them

Usually around the first part of August the grain would be ripe and ready for harvest. Dad would pull out the grain binder, oil all the parts, gears and pulleys. Sharpen the sickle and make sure the binder canvases were in good condition. Sometimes mice would find a place to chew and it would need repair. This prep work would often take a couple of days.

The binder twine came four or six bundles to a sack. There were two compartments on the binder each holding a twine bundle. The two were tied together so the farmer wouldn't run out of twine so fast.

The grain binder was a magical machine. He would hook up the team of horses to the binder and head for the fields. His first trip around the field was a test run. A time to make sure all the settings were operating correctly and tying the bundles tight enough.

If all went well he would continue. When there were several rounds made, there would be a crew of young boys or neighbors who would start shocking the grain bundles. They would take a bundle in each hand and butt the heads together so that they would stand upright. There were six bundles to a shock, with to bundles laid on top to help shed the rain if there was any before the threshing day.

When this day arrived the farmer would have neighbors who also had threshing jobs to do come over with hay wagons and their team of horses. This was referred to as "exchange help." They came early and would head out to the field. There were always some extra men who would help with the loading of the wagon. When loaded they would go back to the separator and pull in alongside of the feeder. One wagon on each side. Then they would pitch one bundle form each wagon, alternating so there would be a steady pace, but being careful not to overload the separator.

I always encouraged Dad to hire the fellow who had the steam engine that blew the whistle when he came and also when he was done with the job.

If the rig had arrived in the evening there was a possibility that mom would have these men for breakfast. In that case she would fix bacon and eggs, bread, butter and jam and cold cereal. I remember it being corn flakes, because that was the only time we ever had cold cereal at home. Also coffee, milk and cool aid.

Dinners were different. There would be about twelve men in all.
Then we had meatballs or roast beef, boiled potatoes and gravy, cooked carrots or green beans from the garden, pickles, homemade buns, apple pie for desert and again lots of coffee, milk or cool aid.

It was such a good feeling when the day was finished and the separator connected to the steam engine pulled out our driveway, and as he was leaving pulled the whistle two times heading for the next job in the neighborhood.

I ITCHED ALL OVER   by Walt Fluegel

Doris, an older lady read a chapter from her memoirs to fellow writers inspired by a black and white photo of mine. The photo was a farm scene which reminded her of her girlhood.

When Doris was about 12 years old she helped in the grain fields at harvest time. Everybody, including neighbors, shared work to bring the grain to harvest. She described the whole process in detail from the thresher cutting the grain to people stacking the grain into shocks.

As an afterthought to her reading she said, "I itched all over. It was very dusty, grimy work." When she made her comments she began to rub her arms and the back of her neck. Several of us writers suggested Doris should include her itchy and grimy comments into her story. Doris's retelling made some of us wish for a shower as soon as we could get home after the meeting! She never mentioned a shower, but I think she was reminded about using a large wash tub.

Later, Doris wanted to know how and where I took the photo. My B&W photo was a composite from two old Kodachrome slides: shocks of grain from one slide and the thresher from another. Both slides were taken at the same location on the same day but alas, my records are incomplete. I merged the two slides using Photoshop Elements 3 program and converted the image to B&W. Doris wanted four copies for some of her younger relatives who continue to farm. I made sepia prints to give the feeling of an old time photo.

"All of my younger relatives who still farm don't know what we did back then. Now, machines do everything," she said. My photo was an inspiration to Doris who jogged her memory to where she could recount and animate the actual "itchiness" and physical work long forgotten. Doris had no photos of her own but my photo will now be part of her memoirs.

I feel pleased that my composite photo enriched her writing with more detail, more realism, and more understanding. And Doris's story has enriched my life as well.

REMEMBERING DORIS by Denis Simonsen

What Walt Fluegel and many other accomplished photographers do with film, Doris Hanson did with her mind's eye and her words. With these well-oiled tools she crafted stories that were vivid and truthful reflections of her life and the lives of people she knew and deeply cared for. To have the experience of listening to her recollections is a treasure I will hold dearly. Not only because she was able to put on the page detailed descriptions of events and experiences that I am familiar with but her style embeds them in my memory as if they were my own. I'm sure she instilled a similar reaction from many of her other readers. In retrospect I realize that it was not only her writing that created this feeling but other ways in which she projected herself that endured her to me and many others. To say that she is missed is certain but to say that she will be remembered is profoundly absolute.

THE CATTLE CHUTE by Doris Hanson

There weren't many farmers that had a cattle chute when I was young, and neither did my dad. However, our neighbor Ferdie Ortendahl did.

Back in the early days of Trade Lake Township the road that went past our farm was not part of the State Highway 48. In those years there was no equipment to deal with steep inclines. So road builders had to find accessible routes that didn't need so much grading and filling.

This was true up until 1930 when major changes were made to State Highway 48. This highway began at the court house in Grantsburg, being the location of the county seat. It followed along with highway 87 south from Grantsburg approximately five miles. Then it turned east at Lutz's corner. Mr. Lutz had a small convenience store there, where you could buy groceries and also fill your car with gasoline. There's only a sign left there now to identify the landmark.

The road continued east past the Bass Lake School. When it came to the Albert Ryss property it made the first large curve to the south, thus leaving the house and farm buildings on the west side of the road and Albert's blacksmith shop on the east side of the road.

As it headed south, it made a small dip then up again only to go down a steep hill. Here is where 48 made a left turn onto what we now know as Spook Drive. It continued on around a curve and then another curve before it straightened out and came out at the top by Ziemer's farm. Here it turned left again, down the hill into the busy Village of Trade Lake. When it reached Albert Baker's house it made a right turn past the Confectionaries store over the Trade River Bridge past the Roller Mill that was powered by the dam nearby.

The road continued south for a short distance then around the mill pond and up past the Trade Lake Graded School No.5.

Starting about 1928 plans were made to make many changes on this stretch of road. Around 1930 workers were busy with the reconstruction of 48. The large curve had been put in at the Ryss's farm, and instead of going east at the bottom of the steep hill (on Spook Drive) it went straight south following the township road to Ortendahl's farm. Here the second large curve was to be constructed. It was very hilly in through there and the layout of the curve made it impossible for Ferdie's cows to get from the barn to the pasture, thus making it necessary for the state to build a cattle chute.

The next large curve was at Trade Lake. There the road made a curve from Lloyd Swanberg's gasoline station crossing over the Trade River where a new cement bridge had been constructed. Connecting with 48 where it came out from the village and curved around the mill pond and instead of following 48 up around to the school, a new stretch of road went through

Frank Larson's property with a small curve at the top of the hill. Once again it joined 48 and headed south to Four Corners where another smaller curve was made.

Going east a short distance the road again veered off to the right and down the hill over the Trade River again, meandering around Round Lake's north shore. Here the road followed along close to the lake. There used to be a nice flat space on the north side right across the road from the lake. Here gypsies would camp in tents on their way passing through this area. I have been told that there was a sign on a tree near the lake: "Linger Longer." No doubt someone thought this to be a very peaceful place to camp.

As we leave scenic Round Lake and go up the hill, we make another large curve by passing the Round Lake School. The road continues on but makes one more small turn to the east where it heads straight for the Polk County Line. Yes, there was a lot of road construction during those years, making it a much better highway to travel on.

But back to the cattle chute. A neighbor recently told me that they used washed sand to build the chute. I wonder what the reason was for that.

Ferdie's daughter Barbara and I were good friends. She was one year ahead of me in school, but we shared a lot of the same interests. As we grew older we found pleasure walking in the woods. We would also find it exciting to go down to the chute and hide. When cars or trucks came by, it would send a rumble through the whole tunnel. Then when we would talk or sing we would sound so funny we couldn't help but giggle!

The chute was fairly high. A person could easily walk through standing upright, and the cows could walk through single file with space to spare on either side.

When there was a heavy rain there would be water in the chute that made it messy for the cows and the farmer to wade through. Usually he would see that all the cattle were headed through first, he would then walk the rest of the way on the road back to the barn.

The chute is still there, unnoticed by speedy travelers on highway 48. But when I go by it, I still think back to the time when we were young and the simple fun we created in that cattle chute

AT THE WEDDING by Doris Hanson

Three Little Flower Girls, all dressed alike,
Waiting their turn down the aisle to take a hike
Baskets of rose petals they carry with pride
To create a pretty path on which to usher the bride.

The first little flower girl came slowly down the aisle
then spotted her mom and made a quick exit, to be at her arm.
The second little flower girl went on to the front
And set herself down on the platform kerplunk!

She looked in her basket and to her surprise,
Where in the bottom more petals she spied
So quickly overturned her basket with glee
And petals all over the floor we could see.

At the front of the church stood the pastor so stately and tall,
With a look on his face that made us wonder in awe
What does he see that makes his face quiver?
That strange look, is making me shiver.

I whisper to Mary Ann, 'What's going on?"
           "I don't know," came her reply!
For us to look behind, we didn't think proper,
But why is the pastor looking so awkward?

Finally the ring bearer, a handsome young lad
Wearing white shirt and tie, with a vest of soft green,
           black shoes and trousers, sees someone he knows
Then leaves the aisle to be by his dad

The third little flower girl was not yet on her way,
Oh my goodness, I wonder what is the delay
Is she crying, is she sick, is she hurt, is she shy?
There is definitely something that has gone awry

What seemed like forever, to us seated in front?
We felt helpless and nervous beyond expectation
Whatever it is I hope it's not serious or bad
This is a celebration, not a time to be sad!

At last the Maid of Honor appeared.
With a smile on her face that reached ear to ear.
She was holding the hand, of the flower girl so fair
Who had thought it her job to pick up the petals lying there?

She had sat on the carpet without any worry
And picked petals one by one, no need to hurry
Into her basket she gently placed them.
Isn't that sweet what her thoughts had been?

Now the father proceeded with the bride by his side
He was strong, yet letting go wasn't easy
The bride smiled and kissed him. Then turned to her groom,
And the Wedding proceeded as Love filled the room.

THE UNINVITED GUEST by Doris Hanson

The party date had been set for Sunday July 26, 1986. Relatives and friends had all been notified as to the time and place. All food and preparation had been made. The day arrived beautiful, warm and sunny. What more could a person ask for when having a party? This party was for Tom, Shari's daddy.

At 10 o'clock in the forenoon I was busy putting on tablecloths, setting out dishes and silverware. I have found that the more you have ready before the guests arrive the better the party works. Then out on the yard Amber, the family collie dog, started barking. I knew from the pitch of her bark that she was excited! I looked out the window, but could see no strange car or anything else unusual. I returned to the kitchen, but Amber would not stop barking. I went out to talk to her but she was more excited than ever. With all the commotion she was making, I thought I'd better take another look out on the yard.

"Oh you're so silly Amber," I said to her, "there's no one here." But she only barked all the more and came closer to the house, with her eyes aimed at the huge oak tree that stood just 20 feet west of our kitchen windows. "What is it Amber, why are you barking at the tree?" I looked higher up in the tree, and where the branches begin to spread out, I could see something black, like a big ball of fur.

"What is it Amber?" I asked her. I spoke in a hushed tone. All Amber would do was bark with glee that she had finally gotten me to notice. My body began to shake at the thought of what it might be! Soon it moved and its head turned in my direction.

"Why Amber, it's a bear, at least I think it's a bear!" All Amber would do was keep on barking.

Since bears are not a common thing in our yard, my first thought was that I should show this unusual sight to my granddaughter, Shari. I went back into the house and said, "Come with me Shari, out on the steps, and look at the bear up in the oak tree. That's a bear Shari, look."

Since Shari was only three years old, her reaction to that bundle of fur up in the tree wasn't as I had anticipated. She cuddled her blanket, looked at the tree and then looked at me and said very slowly, "a bear?"

I knew then that it was well for me to get this little girl back in the house and get her interested in something else, so I could hurry out to the barn and get Tom. Certainly he would get excited I thought.

"Tom! Tom!" I hollered, as I entered the barn. "Come quick." The urgency of my voice must have frightened him, for he came on the run with his face white as a sheet, and asked, "What's wrong? "In my breathless voice I said, "There's a bear in the oak tree, come and see, hurry!

24

"There's a what?"

"There's a bear in the oak tree by the window." I said.

"Are you sure?" He questioned.

"Well come and see for yourself." I said maybe it isn't, after all no one has seen a bear on this farm since 1936 and from what I hear tell, it wasn't anywhere near the buildings."

We hurried back to the house. Amber was still barking. Tom had to take only one look to see that it was a bear, and said, "That's a bear all right. Now, why did he have to come today?"

Since we wanted this to be a fun and joyful party, I quickly said, "Maybe he wanted to be part of the entertainment. I can't say that I had really planned on a bear showing up, but then who knows what fun we'll have!"

"Well, I sure hope he didn't invite the rest of the family." Tom said. And I had to agree with that. Then he added, "Let's hope he comes down and leaves before the other people arrive." I don't think that Tom thought it was a very good idea having a bear sitting up in our tree so close to the house when there were going to be so many people with little children here. I could sure understand his reason for that.

"I think I'll call your brother, Glenn. I'm sure they would like to bring Kathy and Jillian over, after all how often do we have a bear in our tree?"

"Yeh, you can do that. They might like to see it before it comes down and runs away. But I better get back to the barn and get the rest of the work done so I can get cleaned up before the people come."

As Tom headed back to the barn, I'm wondering to myself if I should call the neighbor across the road also, maybe they would like to bring their girls over, too? I went in and called Glenn and the neighbors, finished up my work and got Shari and I dressed for the party.

Now that Amber's barking had told us there was a bear in the tree, she kept her vigil on the yard, still barking frequently. Soon Glenn came with his girls. Oh, the excitement of it all. Then the neighbors came with their families.

Shari was so happy to see everybody and announced, "There's a bear in the tree. Come and see!"

There were many pictures taken. People oohed and aahed. We checked this furry creature from all sides. I'm sure the bear wondered what he had done to receive so much attention. He was not very pleased with his popularity. He hissed, he growled, panted and yawned. Swatted his paw at us, would turn first one way then the other, wishing we would get away from there.
More and more people arrived, and the excitement grew.

Shari ran to each car that arrived and greeted every new guest with "There's a bear in the tree, come and see!"

It was time to put burgers and hot dogs on the grill. The aroma of the meat roasting over the fire floated through the air. You could see that the bear would love to come down and have a sample, for he would stand up and turn around, yawn, put his nose in the air, and sniff the tantalizing burgers sizzling to perfection. But then, of course, there was Amber, still keeping her watch.

The burgers and hot dogs were ready, many delicious casseroles and salads were on the kitchen table, plus other sweet things. Everyone ate their lunch and settled back to rest, visit, play yard games and have a softball game. Amber had even given up on her barking and took a cautious rest.

Well, boys will be boys, and don't you suppose someone had saved a few firecrackers just for this event! Bang! Bang! Bang! They exploded. Now, let me tell you, Amber made one bee-line to the house. Someone saw how scared she was and let her in the door. From there she crawled as far as possible under some furniture. We didn't see any more of her for the rest of the afternoon.

A black bear is bad enough, but "Black Cats"—that's just too much! This racket woke the bear also, and he could see that Amber had left her guard.

She stretched, looked around, thinking, maybe this is my opportunity to leave.

"The bear is coming down! The bear is coming down!" the children shouted, and came running into the house! We ladies in the house hurried to the west windows to watch. Some children stood on the top steps close to the door for a quick escape, while the men stood on the ground and watched to see what would happen. Sure enough the bear came down the trunk and looked around, and scooted right up the tree again. Maybe he didn't trust us; maybe he was more afraid of us than we knew. We waited, we watched. He wiggled around up in the tree where he had always felt secure. He stretched, yawned and growled, and soon he decided to make another attempt to come down.

His descent was slow, but as soon as his feet touched the ground and when he didn't hear any barking, he realized that Amber was nowhere around . He slyly wandered away from the tree trunk about ten feet, looked around some more, then relieved himself, turned around and up the tree he went again.

Every one groaned—oh no! Not again! It was getting close to three o'clock and we were all wishing we could see him leave. Once again he started to wiggle around, yawn, and sniff the air and snort. He started to descend down the tree, everyone was real quiet and still. I don't think the leaves on the tree even moved. On the ground at last, he kept easing his way westward from the tree and people. When he felt he was a safe distance from us, he put his legs into high gear and ran as fast as he could. We watched him lumber across the new- mown hay field and over to the neighbor's cow pasture until we couldn't see him anymore.

That was the last we saw of our "Uninvited Guest." What a birthday party!

THE PEA VINERY by Doris Hanson

Today there are only shell like remains that stand idle here and there around the countryside, reminders of the old pea vineries that were used back in the 1930's and early 1940's.

27

In the early spring a field man from the Stokely Company would contact the farmers in the area. This was their opportunity to sign a contract with Stokelys for the number of acres they would like to plant for the canning company that season. The farmers would prepare their fields. Then the field man would come check the fields to see that they were in the best possible condition for planting and set the date when the peas would be planted.

The peas were planted early in the spring. They could tolerate the cool weather and would germinate and grow very well. The field man would come out periodically to check the field to see how the peas were developing in their pods. Usually Dad's peas were planted so they would be ready for harvest the early days in July. We had to hope it didn't rain or the harvesting might not take place.

The morning of harvest we were up before 4:00 a.m. Dad had a quick cup of coffee, a sandwich and some cookies to start his day. After that he hitched the horses to the horse-drawn hay mower, and then left for the field. My mother, brother and I also had some food to eat before we left the house. We carried with us water jugs, three-tine hay forks and diluted citron oil bug lotion. The bugs were most likely sleeping but with all the cutting and noise disturbing them, we were sure they would find us as an excellent target for their breakfast.

What a beautiful cool, fresh start for a heavy work day. In the sky the stars were still shining with a full moon lighting our way through the woods and over to the pea field. There was such a calm, quiet, stillness in the air. The frogs and birds were still sleeping and the heat of yesterday had left a fragrant combination of damp moss, ripe wild berries and pine trees.

By the time we got to the field Dad had cut a couple rounds. We started to pitch the row he had cut closest by the fence onto the second row he cut. The same was done with the third row forked unto the fourth row, and on it went through the whole field.

The trucks and loader arrived about 6:30 a.m. ready to load and haul the pea vines to the vinery. Our peas were taken to the Paulson vinery located on South Williams Road about three fourths of a mile north of State Highway 48.

The way I remember it at the vinery, the trucks pulled in closely to the conveyer belts. Here the men unloaded the vines. Now they were on their way into the threshing machine, with the vines coming out on a conveyor belt going to the outside where a silage stack was being formed.

The nice luscious green vegetables rolled down the table where a divider could be moved from one side to the other. There were two gray boxes at the end of this table. The peas would roll into the box and when it was full, the divider was moved so the peas would roll into the other box. This procedure continued until the truck was filled with boxes of shelled peas. The truck was ready then to deliver these boxes to the Stokely Canning Company at Frederic.

The silage stack would stand there all summer and since this stuff was green and juicy it would ferment and become similar to corn silage. When colder weather arrived, there were men from Stokelys who would come and open the stack. The farmers who had raised peas were notified, and for a small fee they could buy a trailer load and bring home this silage for their cows. The amount you would be allowed depended on how much acreage you had planted.

The commotion that took place in the barn when dad came home with our small two-wheel trailer load of silage and pulled up by the silo room door was unbelievable. The aroma, to put it mildly, was horrible. But the cattle went berserk! They would bellow, stretch and shake in their stanchions almost to the point of breaking something, all the while their tails switching back and forth, eager to get at this delightful treat. Long after they had finished eating their portions they kept licking and licking the spot where the treat had been.

From this display of eagerness, I know for sure that even the cows enjoy variety in their meal now and then.

THE DRESSER by Doris Hanson

I'm sure you have heard the old saying, "If these walls could talk, what a story they would tell." Well, I'm a dresser that would like to share my story with you.

For many years I lived with a nice lady and her husband. When they were newly-married and didn't have many pieces of furniture, they saw me in a store display window and the lady fell in love with me. They needed a dresser for their bedroom. The tall dark-haired, blue-eyed gentleman could tell how much his wife longed for me, so he bought me and gave me to his wife as a birthday present. This was way back in 1892. I was so happy when they hauled me home in the back of their buggy. It was a bumpy ride, yet I could tell they were going to take good care of me.

After several years and nine children later, sadness came to their home when the husband became ill and died. The lady, in her advanced age, didn't like to live all by herself so she took me and a few of her necessary belongings and went to live with one of her daughters.
The lady wanted to brighten me up, so she painted me a light green. I really felt special then. The lady put a nice dresser cloth on top of me. Here she placed a comb clothes brush, a pink pressed-glass powder box with a pink powder box with a glass cover. Also a bottle of some nice-smelling perfume. This perfume that she used every time she went to visit her friends. It was so nice to be taken care of so well.

One day I heard the other family members talking around the dining table. They were so sad. I couldn't figure it out. Then I realized that my lady wasn't there anymore. I wondered, what will become of me? Who will want me and take care of me?

There were young girls at this house where I was staying, and they liked me and dressed me up with pictures of their friends. I felt so young and useful again. Then another strange thing happened. Soon the girls had graduated from high school and were out working and saving their money. They wanted to buy a new dresser, one that was larger with more drawer space for their clothes. That was all fine and dandy, but what was going to become of me? There will be no room for me anywhere around here!

The girls asked their aunt if she wanted me. She said she didn't have any space in her house. Then the girls asked if maybe her daughter-in-law, who had four young children, would be able to find use for me. And so it was, I was moved over and placed upstairs in her house. This became the dresser of the youngest boy. To add a little child-like look to me, the lady painted the front of my drawers. The top drawer was painted a bright red, the middle one a soft yellow, and the bottom a very pretty blue. Even if this sounds crazy, it made me feel good.

I had a mirror, but it was never put on me because of too little space, and later was sold at a Friday night auction at Falun, Wisconsin. I've often wondered who bought my mirror. It would be nice to have it back with me.

Years went by, and as the boys became older, they left home to attend college or get married. When one of the married boys had their first child, his mother asked if they would like to use me for keeping the baby clothes in. The parents didn't have much in the line of storage space so were happy to come and get me.

After a few years this young couple moved to another city where he had found employment. Unfortunately, I was left behind. Then some new renters moved into the house and didn't want me or need me. They moved me to one of the outside buildings where several other items were stored. Oh, the winters were so cold and the summers were so hot and muggy. A farmer, who lived nearby, stored hay in this building for the winter. That made me dusty and I felt so dirty. Then someone stored muskrat traps in my drawers. I felt like a mess. There I was all by myself. I was so lonesome, I felt like crying.

Then one day I had a visitor. This made me happy and I tried to look my very best. The visitor muttered to herself so I couldn't really tell what she was saying, but it sounded something like she thought I could be fixed up. A few days went by and then a couple young fellows with a pickup truck came and picked me up. Oh my, to get out in the sunshine again feels so warm and good. Then I wondered "Where are they taking me, it sure is a bumpy ride!"

After what seemed like several miles the pick-up came to a stop in front of a red shed. Oh dear! Don't tell me I'm going to be stuck in this place! Sure enough, the fellows got out of the pickup and one fellow grabbed a hold of me on one side and the other fellow took hold of me on the other side, and away I went into this shed. When they left and closed the door it became really dark in there. This was scary.

The next day the lady came out and opened the door. Aha! She carried lots of rags and a can of something, some scrapers and a screwdriver. What in the world is she going to do with all that? She took one drawer at a time and brought me out in the fresh air and sunshine. She took the screwdriver and removed the drawer pulls. She opened the can of something gooey and spread that cold stuff all over the front of the drawer. It didn't smell very good, but when the lady took the scraper and pushed it across me it took off all the gooey stuff plus the old green paint, revealing my lovely oak structure beneath. This felt pretty good. I liked this bath I was getting.

Day by day the lady would do more and more cleaning. She cleaned me both inside and out. Then there was sanding to do, so the finish would be smooth and ready for varnishing. When the lady came with the varnish can and brush, I really started to sparkle. I could hardly believe I was the same dresser that had been green. Since I didn't have a mirror the lady went to a Target store and found one that was about the right size, 18 inches by 32 inches, with the right color wood frame. The lady thought it was pretty with the three rows of decorative etching on the glass.

The lady has a nice dresser scarf on me now. Also a fancy comb, brush and a hand-held mirror set. I feel so good that the lady has me in her house and I greet all her company with a smile when they take a peek to check their hair and lipstick.

Maxine E Fluegel (1935 – 2010)

Although Maxine was born in McHenry ND she spent her childhood in Clearwater and Buffalo, MN. After high school graduation, Max became a secretary where she soon met Walt in the Microbiology Department of the then North Dakota Agricultural College at Fargo. They married and moved to Seattle while Walt was trying to get advanced degree. They finally settled in Duluth MN when Walt became a UMD biology professor.

Max was a stay at home mom until Margo and Grey were old enough to allow Max to get a job as Decorator at the local J C Penney store. She excelled there to where the company wanted her to set up and conduct a class in Bloomington MN to teach other Decorators. After a few years of teaching hundreds, Max decided to go into business for herself and this is where her dormant writing blossomed. As part of her business she wrote a regular newsletter for her customers. In the meantime she also got lots of practice in being chief editor for Walt's' writings.

When Max and Walt moved to Grantsburg they began to contribute to the activities of the Writers for several years until cancer took her away.

Maxine loved to do crossword puzzles and found one that had DUO-RHYMING answers. The first cluster came directly from the crossword book but the Q&A section came from both of our thoughts. The whole list was sent to a friend. I found these in our archives residing in a file I had not seen for years. Perhaps they would make a "filler" in some white space. I suspect that only crossword lovers would understand what this is all about.

Question	Answer
cheerleading coach?	rootertutor
crybaby?	minorwhiner
crazed pundit?	balmyswami
pusillanimous know-it-all?	cravenmaven
foxy female?	cannygranny
devout defender?	holygoalie
tiny terror?	riledchild
tree surgeon?	arborbarber
priggish sot?	stewedprude
mother's sister garment?	auntiespanties
most intelligent scribe?	brighterwriter
tree climbers jewelry?	squirrelspearls
more bark than bite?	benigncanine
office worker greeting?	hellosteno
bedroom attendant?	sleeperkeeper
dirty bovine	messybessi

SUMMER IS A PAINTING by Maxine Fluegel

The house is quiet, the garden serene
Summer is sitting on a canvas of green
Painted with blossoms in colorful hues
Brilliant reds, yellows, oranges--soft blues.
A cardinal warbles his deep throaty song
While chickadees bustle and chatter along.
As bees are a-buzzing on flowers a-sway,
The kids down the street are laughing at play.
Summer is a painting where memories abound.
It is here that the brush strokes of life may be found.

BYLINE by Maxine Fluegel

1 X 1 we wait patiently in line,
restless when there are more than 9.

2 X 2 Noah filled his ark--
pushing on into the dark.

A 3 X 5 card is standard fare
to jot a recipe to share.

If a 4 X 4 is a 4-wheeled drive,
loan me 1 and I'll give you 5.

Photos are 3 X 5, 4 X 6, 8 X 10, 11 X 17 sizes--
the bigger the prints, the more the prizes.

8 1/2 X 11 are letter size papers,
8 1/2 X 14 are for legal capers.

9 X 12, a standard rug,
unless the weaver was with the jug.

So, when feet and inches become metric wonders,
Let's hope I'm already 6 feet under!

MAKE A MIRACLE! by Maxine Fluegel

I have had a reasonably successful year, mostly pleasant and occasionally exciting. In fact, in January I made a miracle.

I was driving in the far right lane on a busy one-way street. Gradually, I realized a car on my left was slowly drifting into my lane, much too close for comfort. I touched my brakes and pulled as close to the icy snow bank as I dared with seconds to spare before we would have collided.

There was no signal of the driver's intention to come into my lane. Clothing hung on a rod across the driver's side of the back seat. Two boxes were piled high on the passenger side in the back. She was oblivious to what had almost happened. There was a sticker on the back of her car, "Expect a miracle".

The irony of the situation struck me and I said aloud, "Lady, I just gave you your miracle!"

Later, I realized that when we 'expect a miracle' we often have no control over what happens. We wait for someone else to give us what we want or need. However, if we 'make a miracle' we plan ahead for what we want to accomplish. Then we need to take an active part in making it occur-- whether it be a healthful life, sustaining friendships, overcoming shyness or reluctance or procrastination or succeeding in a career.

So go ahead. Try it. Go out and make yourself a miracle!

STUMPY by Maxine Fluegel

Several chipmunks visit our flower gardens. They feed from our elevated, flat, open bird feeder which sits on an abandoned chair. Three summers ago, we noticed half of the tail of one of the chipmunks was missing and the end was bloody. We nicknamed him 'Stumpy'.

We watched his progress as the end of the tail healed quickly. The loss has not impaired his ability to find food, or to run, or hop, or climb trees. When he is on the feeder, he chases away other chipmunks who want to jump up on it and others chase him if they are there first. Occasionally, two of them race after each other around the yard and garden and up and down the trees. Finally, they catch each other and roll round and round on the ground. In a few moments the tussle is over and they may both jump onto the feeder and eat peacefully side by side.

Stumpy has two favorite resting places by our log house. He sits and cleans himself and eats seeds on one of the protruding logs at the corner of the house. The other spot is on the edge of the dining room window box, where he watches the world go by. Sometimes he buries seeds amongst the flowers in the soil of the box and he scampers through the plants.

Once when we went on a two-day trip, we returned to find the bird feeder empty. We were hungry and decided to eat lunch before we filled the feeder. As soon as we sat down to eat at the dining room table, Stumpy jumped up into the window box and scurried onto the window ledge. He was very close to the window and chattered insistently at us as if to say, "When do I get fed around here!"

Many times over the last few years Stumpy has visited the window box, drowsed on the ledge or looked up at us as we eat lunch. My husband started "talking" to him through the window glass and started calling him our "little friend." We say to each other during the day, "Your little friend is gorging himself on seeds again. There goes that little vacuum cleaner sucking up seeds."

Stumpy inflates his cheek pouches with seeds, then jumps off the feeder, scampers beneath and through the flowers in the garden, hops, bounces and "floats on air" over the grassy expanse into the woods at the edge of the lawn. Once we watched him bury sunflower seeds at the edge of the garden. We dug them up and there were thirty-two seeds, others tell us they have counted seventy-two from their chipmunk's stash. Stumpy and the others collect and bury seeds most of the day until all seeds are gone.

A few weeks ago a fox with beautiful rusty and black and silver fur came through our yard. He visited most early evenings for about a week. We have not seen the fox for some time now. Also, we have not seen Stumpy. We wonder if he was eaten by the fox. He was a survivor, but perhaps his days were numbered. We will miss him.

Walt shared this photograph with me and with his permission I have added this poem here, which I thought Maxine would have enjoyed. Denis

TEETER TOTTER by Denis Simonsen

We stop
His chipmunk path has intersected mine
His cheeks chuck full of tomorrows
My wheel barrow piled high with winter comfort
His eyes sparkle a challenge
My smile reveals a curiosity
Time stands still

I take a step
He darts between my legs

I turn and watch him
Tail held high

Pumping his furry body towards safety
His earth home

A lukewarm cup of coffee
Takes the bite out of a chilling wind

I sit and contemplate my own journey
Across the lawn
From woodpile to porch
And hope that nothing larger than myself
Keeps me from my destination

MEMORIES OF MAXINE by Bob MacKean

I wish I had gotten to know Maxine better. I only had the chance to meet her when she came to our club meetings. I regret the opportunities I missed to meet a very extraordinary lady.
When the news came out of her passing, one memory became vivid and precious.

She came to a meeting with Walter and sat away from the group where she could observe. When it was Walter's turn to speak, he began his in-depth reading on the topic and as I listened I noticed that Maxine was listening more intently than anyone at the table. Her eyes were glued on Walter with a pride and respect, I can only dream about getting when I speak. The love and respect was evident on her face. She truly loved the man who was speaking.

I sometimes see that look on my wife's face when I read to her. Nothing lifts my heart and it keeps me going. Walter is a very lucky man to have known such love.

MY ULTIMATE TASTE SENSATION by Maxine E. Fluegel

The last time I ate my favorite chocolatey food was on the afternoon of September 6, 1997. It was my birthday and my husband knew I was yearning for a Bridgeman's Turtle Sundae, a lovely concoction of vanilla ice cream topped with hot chocolate, butterscotch syrup, pecans, whipped cream and a maraschino cherry. But, alas, it was to be my final Turtle Sundae--Bridgeman's Ice Cream Parlor closed its remaining stores and, later, I developed an unresolved and potentially dangerous allergy to all milk and dairy products.

Nevertheless, my memory of the Turtle Sundae is as vivid today as my enjoyment of it was in the past. My addiction to it began in the mid-70 when I was an in-home decorator for J. C. Penney in Duluth, MN. After making particularly large sales for draperies and carpet, I began rewarding myself with a turtle sundae at Bridgeman's which was in an adjacent mall to Penney's. There were even occasions when all I had for lunch was a Turtle Sundae. After all it was nutritious--chocolate for mental well-being, cream for healthy bones, maraschino cherry as fruit, pecans with healthy oils and flavored syrups for extra carbohydrates!

Now, those pleasures are in the past; although, as I recall it, every mouthful of those wonderful sundaes was sheer joy. Here is the story of my ultimate taste sensation.

The waitress delivers my Turtle Sundae to the table. She sets it on a clean, white paper napkin because the melting ice cream is already running down the sides of the tall, clear sundae glass. The whole thing is absolutely beautiful--ice cream and thick, creamy dark brown hot chocolate and caramel-colored butterscotch syrup are sprinkled with toasted, salted, chopped pecans. The glass gives me a peek at each item and fills my memory with their mouthwatering creaminess and sweetness and their smooth delicious flavors. A dollop of whipped cream and a shiny, luscious red maraschino cherry with an attached stem tops the entire offering.

Carefully, I grasp the stem of the cherry, lay its red crispness into my mouth and bite down. The juicy berry spills it's liquid onto my tongue, spreading the cool, sweet juice down my throat. Gently, I pick up the slim, long-handled spoon, savoring the moment when I dip into the edge of the whipped cream, gently push the spoon down through the pecans and into the rich, smooth hot chocolate, through the butterscotch and into a small bit of ice cream. Now, I lift the spoon carefully, trying not to spill the concoction down the outside of the glass. Slowly and deliberately the spoon goes into my mouth. There is a noticeable peak for each flavor and texture--the fluffiness and oiliness of whipped cream, the cool creaminess of ice cream, the thick coating of chocolate on the tongue, the slick sweet caramel of butterscotch, and the salty, crunchy, oily flavor of pecans. It is absolutely delicious! Over and over I repeat these rituals, watching the ingredients blending into each other until the glass is completely empty and the spoon tinkles in the bottom of the glass.

What a delightful experience. And what a wonderful memory!

NICE LITTLE MESSAGES by Maxine Fluegel

Sometimes we worry that nothing good happens in the big world around us. Many occurrences seem beyond our control and often beyond our interest. Nevertheless, when we look closely at our daily lives, we often see that we receive little messages which help us feel good about ourselves and the other people who touch our lives.

On a very simple level, have you ever had the agreeable feeling which comes from opening a door for another person or when they open it for you? There is a little bond connecting the two of you for a few seconds out of a busy day and you both go on with a little smile.

Whenever you tell a salesclerk how much you appreciate her help, you send a little message which brings both of you a feeling of satisfaction.

Should a friend telephone after a long gap, tell her how wonderful it is to hear her voice again--surely this brings joy to both of you.

There are a number of steps we can take to enjoy life more fully: If we allow extra time, maybe an hour, to get ourselves ready for work, shopping or an appointment, we may have time to drive on quiet streets instead of freeways, when possible. As we travel, we can look for beauty in our environment, take time to savor a sunrise, a sunset, beautiful trees and landscapes, an attractive building or whatever appeals to our senses.

We can also do things for others. Give our children more hugs. It smoothes the way to understanding and happiness. We can clean house for our married children with youngsters thus allowing them time to do the other things they don't have time to do. It will give all of us great satisfaction and contentment.

If we have a friend whose husband/wife has been ill, volunteer to sit with the ill spouse while the other shops, goes to an appointment or has a few hours to relax.

We can volunteer to baby sit for a young couple whose parents live out of the area. A little time by themselves will surely recharge the young couple's batteries.

As you can see, every day there are many messages which have the potential for making us feel good about ourselves and our world.

We need to seek out these nice little messages and create and send some of our own.

A LINE IN THE SAND by Maxine Fluegel

It was one of those bright, sunny Saturdays--a perfect day for a picnic at Merriwether Park. Graham was a small town in the middle of Missouri. On a nice day many people came to the park. The Adams and Brown families, who lived next to each other, liked to picnic together. Each had boys nine years old--Mikey Adams and Joey Brown. Mikey had a black dog, Laddie, who loved to romp in the water and sniff at junk on the beach.

Today Mikey and Joey worked together to build an elaborate sand castle. They made flags for tops of the spires from sticks and tiny pieces of junk found on the beach. The castle had a moat around the outside edges. They brought their toy knights and horses and people from home to play with in the castle.

When they tired of castle play, the boys dug a deep hole in the sand close to the lake. After a few minutes, it filled with water from the lake and they floated their toy boats on it.

As the day wore on, the boys grew short with each other. Mikey complained, "That yellow boat is mine. Get your hands off it." Joey put Mikey's boat back in the water, but then he kicked sand into the water and the boat sank. Mikey jumped up and darted to a smooth area of sand near the hole. He dragged his toe in the sand and drew a deep, straight line from the lake back towards the picnic table. "See this line? You stay on your side and I'll stay on mine--or else!"

"Or else what?" Joey was already up close to the line.
"You'll see! Just try it once!"

Joey poked at Mikey across the line and caught him on the elbow. Mikey swung his arm towards Joey's chest and Joey grabbed it with his left arm.

"Who do you think you are swinging at me, I'll...."

Just then Laddie came out of the lake and stopped between the two boys. Quickly he gave a tremendous shake of his body from his head down to his tail. Water was thrown off his back and tail and pelleted the boys. Mikey and Joey gasped for air as they grabbed for Laddie and wrestled him on to the sand. There was yelling and barking and giggling. Wet blobs of sand stuck to Laddie's fur and stuck to the boys' legs and arms and tummies.

Just as the boys differences disappeared with the sudden burst of playful activity, so the line in the sand was soon scuffled away.

LIVING IN CLEARWATER by Maxine Fluegel

When I was a kid my brother, Gary, and I used to take our old beat up, rusty wagon out to the grassy banks and ditches outside of town to pick up glass pop bottles thrown out of car windows. We hauled them back to town to Mr. Ness's grocery store. He gave us 3¢ for each bottle.

After we saved enough money, we bought my favorite candy, round hard licorice with one end flattened like a glass cutter. Gary liked round bubble gum with cartoons inside the wrapper. That was my second choice and sometimes Mom gave us a few extra pennies, so we could get more than one choice. After we got back home, we ate our candy and chewed our bubble gum sitting close together with neighborhood kids near the edge of the sidewalk in the grass out front of our house. When we wore out our bubble gum, we wound it around our bare toes or stretched it like sling shots or twirled it around our heads like we saw Roy Roger's or Gene Autry's lariats do at the double feature movies in Annandale every Saturday night.

Clearwater was a very small town which had one grocery store, a post office, a funeral parlor which was closed--except when someone died which wasn't very often, a lumber yard, a locker plant, a liquor store with an eating place, and a beer parlor with a dance hall upstairs which was used on Saturday nights and for wedding dances.

When I was eleven or twelve, my folks took me and my best friend, Kathy, to our first dance at the beer parlor at the end of the main street.

At intermission we went to the outhouse with my Mom and some of her friends. It was the first time I saw my mother smoke a cigarette. I was shocked--Mom smoking? Most women I knew didn't smoke in those days. I found out later that Mom had smoked since she was a teenager, but she only smoked when she was alone in the outhouse.

It took me a while to regain my respect for Mom. I suppose this incident happened around the time I found out there was no Santa Claus. This from the only people I'd depended on for so long for everything. My folks were not to be trusted for a while!

Most people in Clearwater didn't have indoor plumbing, just a one or two seater outhouse out back which was stinky in the summer, scary at night, and too cold in winter. So you held it too long. I've never been right since then.

My folks moved a lot but we lived in Clearwater five or six years. When I remember growing up, I remember this place most of all.

We made good friends here. My best friend, Kathy, lived across the street from us. I have not had a best friend since then and I have never seen Kathy again since we left Clearwater to move to Buffalo where I started high school, ninth grade in those days.

I was in eighth grade before I got eyeglasses. Mom discovered I needed them one day when she asked me what time it was. I was on the opposite end of the kitchen across from the clock. I told her I'd go over to see the time. She was amazed that I couldn't see the clock across the room. It was not long before I was taken to the eye doctor over in the big city of Buffalo to test my eyes. Sure enough I was very nearsighted and needed glasses badly. In school I always liked to sit in the front seat, so seeing the blackboard had been no problem.

In two weeks my new eyeglasses were ready to pick up in Buffalo. When I got home I went outside to play. It was spring and the grass in the yard had been beautifully soft and green when I left home that morning. Now, I saw individual blades of grass! What a joy!

Everything around me popped out at me. My brother's face was sharp and clear. Nothing was blurry. The sun shone brightly among the tree branches which were dark and sharp. From that time forward I never took off my glasses except to clean them or when I went to bed. It was new world for me to explore! I was thirteen years old.

MY FIRST JOB by Maxine Fluegel

When I graduated from high school in 1953 I knew I would be a secretary. Many of my courses were oriented in that direction--shorthand, typing, bookkeeping, correct letter writing and office procedures. While in school, the principal, for whom I had been an assisting secretary for a year, told me I would probably not be able to make it at a college or university because of my parent's being poor, my own shyness, and of my having lived out in the country for much of my life. This even after I was graduated in the top ten of 120 students and after being called "smarty pants" by most fellow students all during those years. But I believed the principal, he must know better than anyone. So I knew I was destined to become a willing worker oiling the cogs of society. Therefore, I diligently sent my resumes to job offers in the area where I lived with my parents which included Rush City, Pine City and as far away as St. Cloud in Minnesota.

The first and only interview I had became my first real job after graduation. It was as a secretary for the Pine County Welfare Board in Pine City. I took dictation and typed information into client folders from the three social workers, Mr. Ole Wangensteen, Mr. Ed Lasky and one other older gentleman. They were all gray-haired and paunchy. There were two other young women typists with whom I went out to lunch and supper. We went to movies together and socialized in general.

But the most interesting person to me was the Executive Secretary of the Board, Mrs. Portia Gunn. She was very tall with deep silver gray hair rolled into a rim around the back and to the sides of her head, her hair pulled flat and straight from a part in the middle of her forehead. She had a very pleasant manner, moved about quickly and quietly, made decisions easily and cajoled the social workers to do their best. Little did I know that Mrs. Gunn was far ahead of most women of the day in her position with the Welfare Board. But I think I quietly admired her physical carriage and her quiet skills as Executive Secretary.

Sometimes a client would call the office complaining they had not received their monthly stipend or they needed something special. One older woman called often, making a pest of herself. She had not received her special undergarment device (a girdle) and wanted Mr. Lasky to make sure she had an order for her bread with no gluten.

My job was an interesting and easy one. I discovered that I had a good mind for remembering details and could anticipate needs of workers and the Executive Secretary. I also found I was a good organizer and learned about the welfare business quickly.

All in all I found I enjoyed being a secretary and stayed at this job for about a year until I decided to move to Fargo, North Dakota to work in the Microbiology Department at North Dakota Agricultural College as the only Secretary/Typist in the department.

It was here that I began to understand that my high school principal had been wrong about my not making it at a college or university. I found the professors and students and the university setting to be a very stimulating, interesting and understandable place for me. But that is another story.

At each meeting of the Northwest Regional Writers, we share a "tidbit," a quotation about writing or reading. Throughout our book we share some of these with you.

TIME ON A RIVER by Mary Jacobsen

Father Marquette knew it by one of its Indian names, the Meskonsing, but a misreading in Marquette's journal caused Guillaume de L'Isle to call the river "Ouisconsin"on his map of 1674.

Almost 300 years later, in the early 1960s, my husband and I, with two of our small daughters, began our three-day adventure on that river, now known as the Wisconsin. We put in at its source at Lac Vieux Desert, a small lake bordering the state of Wisconsin and Michigan's Upper Peninsula. Our packed canoe contained sleeping bags, a tent, a small alcohol camping stove, food, water, flashlights, and the four of us. We were ready to begin paddling on the narrow, winding Upper Wisconsin River and to camp in the woods along the way.

Although we were within walking distance of the highway much of the time, we didn't see another human being the entire trip. We felt so far from modern civilization we wouldn't have been surprised to meet French explorers or fur traders seeking adventure and profit. We imagined encountering, in their birch bark canoes, Indians of yore with eagle feathers in their hair and beaded doeskin moccasins on their feet. We wondered what we might offer them in exchange for their colorfully decorated baskets heaped with wild blueberries. We tried to think what we ourselves would have been carrying for trade—pots? pans? knives? beads?

Formed thousands of years earlier by the melting ice of the receding glacier, the river continues its journey through forests of pine, maple, poplar, and willow. As we continued *our* journey, we became attuned to the river's character and its surroundings. We felt at one with nature on each of these perfect August days.

Clouds, like heaps of whipped cream, floated lazily in the blue sky, and we breathed in the scent of water and pine. As though mesmerized, we watched the quiet drama of a dry leaf as it drifted from a willow tree and floated along the leisurely moving water. Occasionally, our attention would be caught by a fish as it leapt from the water to snap at an insect and then vanish, leaving ever-widening rings on the surface.

An eagle soared overhead, just beyond the canoe as though leading us. The children spoke in whispers, and we glided slowly past a doe and her fawn who had come to the river to drink. Then our eagle left us to navigate for ourselves. Soon, or maybe much later (minutes and hours had lost their meaning), we paddled around a bend to see a Great Blue Heron near the tree-lined shore standing as still as a statue, the water softly rippling around its tall, thin legs while it waited for the approach of a careless fish. As though suddenly remembering a pressing obligation, the heron lifted its huge wings and took off, its long legs trailing behind.

"Maybe it's a mother and she went to take care of her babies, "Ann Louise surmised. Lisa thought the heron was tired of standing and needed exercise.

A good idea for us too. Sitting in the canoe for such a long time was tiring, and though we'd taken a few siestas along the way, we willingly paddled ashore and lashed the canoe to a tree. As the sun tinted the sky gold and roseate, we ate our supper of hot dogs and instant cocoa and talked about all we had seen that day. The sky darkened, and we watched a crescent moon rise above the trees. We found the Big Dipper among the stars that sprinkled the evening sky and wished we could name the other constellations. Later, we lay in our tent waiting for sleep and listened to owls, whippoorwills, frogs, insects—all the mysterious sounds of the night.

In the early morning light, unrestricted by clothing, we swam and splashed as freely in the clear water as though we were the only humans in this special world of ours.

One afternoon, just before entering a narrow passage between a small island and the shore, I noticed a branch hanging low over the water and shouted a warning.

"Duck, everybody, duck!"

All of us ducked as the canoe passed under the branch. All of us, except Lisa. The evidence—a yelp and a thin trickle of blood down her forehead.

"Didn't you hear me shout duck?"

"I looked, but I didn't see any duck."

At the end of our third day, although ready to resume our everyday lives, we reluctantly beached the canoe and walked the short distance through the woods to a roadhouse where we phoned my mother. She met us there and drove us to the river's source where we had parked our car. The drive took twenty minutes.

Although the traffic of explorers, fur traders, Indians in birch bark canoes, and loggers has ended, the river continues to serve as a highway. These days it's barges and pleasure boats that cruise its waters, and picnic tables and public campsites along the way offer accommodations for vacationers.

Our family has experienced many adventures over the years. Yet, those three days of quiet beauty on the Upper Wisconsin River are among the most memorable. We feel fortunate to have been granted, in the river's eventful history, a rare, brief interlude of tranquility.

GUNTHER KILLS COUPLE by Walt Fluegel

"Vern, ... you say Gunther bragged about killing this couple when they came into his house during the night? You say, what was it, last Wednesday? How come the sheriff's office, meaning me, never heard about this until today? That's over a week ago!"

"Honest, sheriff, I heard him brag about it at the grocery store no more than a half hour ago. That's why I hurried over here to tell you. Sounds like a mad man murder."

"What did you really hear Vern? You don't always get your story straight Vern, so tell me who this fellow is. Is this guy that photographer fellow?"

"Yeah, sheriff, that's right, he bragged that he took pictures of the whole thing! He said that he crushed their skulls! He said they were intruders! He got them while they were eating something in the dining room. They came in during the night and that's when he did them under."

"Are you sure you heard him right Vern? You get too excited when you hear people talk. This Gunther guy, you know he is also a writer, and he may be telling stories? You must have overheard him just telling a story. Besides how would he dispose of the bodies?"

"That's right! That's right, sheriff. I remember! He said something about bodies. He said something about getting rid of the bodies by burying them under a pile of leaves in the back yard."

"Come on Vern you have to be kidding me. Have you really seen this guy Gunther up close?"

"Yeah. Sort of a shrimp."

"Look, Vern, the guy could not be more than 120 pounds if that. Besides, he's an old geezer. Can you really see this old guy dragging two bodies out of the house and then burying them? Besides no one reported any missing persons."

"I know sheriff it sounds weird, but when some guys go bonkers something happens to them and they go strange and gain a lot of strength for a short time. I heard how in desperation these little guys can pick up heavy timbers and stuff like that and can't remember what they did or how they did it. I'll tell you sheriff, he sounds like a mad man, he was laughing all the time he told this story."

"Come on Vern, you're letting your imagination get the better of you. I'll tell you what, I'll go pay Gunther a friendly visit."

"If it is a friendly visit, can I go with you sheriff? I can identify him!"

"I know about this guy. You stay here with Deputy Robinson and tell him all you told me, Vern."

"Say Bill, can you take Vern's statement? And Vern, remember all you can so you don't mind if deputy Robinson asks you again to repeat what you told me, and don't leave anything out."

And with that the sheriff gave Deputy Bill Robinson a wink and in return Deputy Robinson raised his eyebrows and motioned Vern to come sit down in the chair next to his desk.

By the time the sheriff entered Gunther's driveway, Gunther put the groceries away and was about to go check the mail. The sheriff parked his car, got out and introduced himself. Gunther asked him if there was anything he could do for him. Just a friendly visit the sheriff said and asked if he was Gunther. Gunther told him he was Gunther.

The Sheriff said he had to make the rounds and wanted to alert people on Johnson Road. He heard reports of intruders.

"Do you have anyone poking around that you don't recognize? Intruders of any kind?"

"Nah, maybe a salesman or a religious guy. The only intruders I get are mice. Hey, if you have the time sheriff I can show you photos of the couple I caught just last week. Want to see them?"

Expecting the world to treat you fairly because you are good is like

expecting the bull not to charge because you are a vegetarian.

Burnett. County Sentinel

IT WASN'T LUCK by Tina Widell

"What a beautiful day," I remarked to Annie. Annie barked in response. I sat at the table with my eggs and English muffin and stared out the window. The ranch was 20 miles from anything. Green grass stretched out beyond mature oaks. I found myself thinking again. I had grown up with a younger sister, but Mom had told us when we were quite young that she'd lost a baby before us.

That baby had been taken by God after only 2 days of life. I thought often of her, wondering what she would be like. I was not like the rest of my family and I wondered if she would have been like me. I shook the thoughts from my head and looked down at Annie.

"Let's take Raven for a ride today." Annie barked again and wagged her long black tail. I put my dishes away and Annie and I walked out to the barn. Raven greeted us with a snort as we came in and Annie barked her good morning. I led Raven out of the barn with Annie trotting around her feet, barking incessantly. Raven was never more than slightly annoyed by the little dog constantly being underfoot and she had become accustomed to the barking. I brushed her black coat until it shimmered in the sun. Then I hitched her up to the small cart and double checked all the straps and buckles. Certain all was in order, I climbed aboard the cart.

"Up!" I commanded Annie. She jumped into the cart. "Ready?" Annie barked. "Let's go!" I called to Raven. Raven snorted and began walking down the long driveway.

"How far shall we go today, ladies?" I asked. Annie barked and Raven neighed loudly, nodding her head. I let out a laugh. "Okay," I said, not sure what I was agreeing to. I sat back a little and let the breeze run its fingers through my hair.

We had been out about an hour at a good trot. I supposed we had gone about 12 miles. Suddenly the sky turned black as night and the wind started to blow hard. Raven stopped. I could not see her but I could tell she was moving around, not sure what to do. Annie barked. She had also blended in with the dark. Then there was a deafening crack of thunder and a bright bolt of lightning. The cart tipped back as Raven reared. She started off at a dead run with the cart right behind her. She was so afraid she could not listen to my commands. She went off the road, into the trees. I screamed as the cart tipped on its side. Raven was caught. Annie fell on top of me. Raven was still wildly scared and confused. I had an incredible pain in my leg. I couldn't move. I whispered to Raven, tried to reassure her but she was terrified. Annie barked.

"Hello!" I heard the woman's voice despite Annie's unrelenting bark.

"Hello!" I shouted back. I saw a vague silhouette approaching.

"SSHH," the stranger said, and both Raven and Annie were silenced and still.

"Wow. You have an incredible way with animals," I said, wincing in pain.

"Thank you," the woman said. "I see you need some help."

"Well, I suppose I do, but what can you do by yourself? My leg is bad, the cart is tipped, the pony is caught….."

"The pony isn't hurt so let me do what I can," she replied. I couldn't see how she did it but she made quick work of untangling Raven who was incredibly calm despite the whipping wind.

"Reach up and grab the other side of the seat. Lift as much of your weight as you can to help me tip the cart upright again."

I did and the cart was easily on 4 wheels again. Raven flinched but stayed calm. The woman took Raven's bridle and started leading her. I didn't know where she was taking us but I rode in silence, wincing only to myself at every bump along the way. After only a few minutes she stopped and tethered Raven to a tree. Annie jumped down from the cart. She and Raven had obviously put complete trust in this stranger and since no human has a better sense of character than animals, I had to trust her too. She helped me down from the cart and let me use her body as a crutch. She took us inside a shack that I had not known was there. She sat me down on the bed. "I'll be right back." After she had gone, I looked around. There wasn't much in here. Just a bed and an end table with a lamp and a phone. The floor was bare cement. Annie jumped up beside me on the bed.

Minutes later the woman returned, leading Raven right into the shack. "I'm sorry," she said. There isn't shelter for her outside and since she will likely be here until long after the storm, she might as well come in. She can't hurt anything."

"Except to leave giant landmines on the floor." I chuckled.

She smiled and waved a hand. "Easily taken care of."
Seeing her face for the first time, I was amazed at how much this woman looked like me. Her hair was the same color, her eyes, nose, even her chin, all looked like mine. I banished the thought from my mind. It wasn't possible-- just my fantasies playing out in my head.

"Help is on the way. They should be here soon."

"You called?"

"Sure. I heard the dog and the crash and knew someone would need something."

"How can I thank you for everything? We are so lucky you were here."

"There is no need for that. Anyone would do it. And it really wasn't luck."

"There is something about you.....You are amazing. You quieted the animals, untangled and unhooked the harness in complete darkness.... Who are you?"

The woman looked at me and smiled. The sound of sirens suddenly blared over the sound of the wicked wind. She looked toward the door. Then looking at me again, she walked backwards toward the door. She did not speak but I heard a voice inside my head whisper,

"Your sister." The door opened and the paramedics rushed in as she vanished from sight. They never saw her. They were talking to me but I

56

stared, stunned, at where she had been standing. It really wasn't luck. My big sister was watching out for us from Heaven.

The significant problems we face today cannot be solved at the same level of thinking we were at when we created them. Albert Einstein

May all your troubles last as long as your New Year's Resolutions

I speak of the New Farm. It is a place in the upcountry about 17 miles from Mount Vernon, New York where "delicate" and /or mischievous boys and girls were sent for a year or two to improve their physical and social beings. The New Farm was operated by the Wartburg Orphan Home in Mount Vernon, New York. The farm provided food for the home and adjacent to the farm up a gradual hill there were two houses, one for the boys and another house nearby for the girls. Mr. and Mrs. Zimmerman originally from Germany, were the house parents for 26 or so boys under their care.

MOHAWKS AND SETTLERS by Walt Fluegel

All of this newness that first summer at the New Farm was absorbed and relished by Gunther, Hendrickson, Larson, Sauer and others. The seemingly aimless walks by the group in the nearby woods edging the east pasture, finding wild grape vines hanging from the overhead branches of taller trees and swinging on these vines until they broke, finding a wide stone fence deep in the woods, wide enough to walk or run on its flat top, jumping from one top rock to another over an occasional gap as if it were a missing sidewalk, all on the way to the shore of Kensico Lake, made for one long summer of glorious, cool, woodsy days. The freedom, the uninhibited exploration and the happiness were deeply absorbed by their souls.

  The older boys gave the message that the stone fence in sight of the lake was a limit. They should not go further, and this was honored when it was explained why. The lake was the New York City water supply. Nobody was allowed to swim in the water or throw anything into it. The trees and bushes grew up to the water's edge. When it rained the night before, there were rivulets to explore in the woods.

One day while wandering home, Gunther, Dressler and Watson stayed behind and dug around in a stream bank. Gunther was fascinated by the soft, pale yellow clay with blue streaks in it. The clay was cool and slippery in his fingers. He called Dressler and they both rubbed the clay on their faces and pretended it was Mohawk Indian war paint. Watson joined in. The pale clay designs showed well against their summer-tanned faces. Before long a voice from up ahead called to keep up.

When Gunther, Dressler and Watson caught up, the others used improvised walking sticks as rifles and they shot toward the Mohawks. It was three braves against many settlers. After this skirmish with the pioneer settlers was over, Byron Hendrickson thought everyone should hurry. He was hungry as usual, and it might be near supper time.

Finally everyone straggled into home territory to the small artificial pond in the woods in sight of the east pasture. The boys' house was located on top of the hill. By looking up the path only the top of the house could be seen. It was near time to stop playing and get ready for supper. The clay on the faces of the Mohawks was dry and began to itch so the Mohawks kneeled on the stones of the pond to wash their faces and rub off the clay.

It was a great mistake for the Mohawks.

It was a great temptation for the renegade settler, Byron Hendrickson. Hendrickson lost his battle with self-control. He had been doing fine all summer at the New Farm. Spontaneity was his trademark in Mt. Vernon. While Gunther was on his knees leaning over the pond and washing his face, Hendrickson gave him a shove.

The pond was at least four feet deep with straight, stone sides. Gunther made one complete somersault into the cool water. When he came up gasping for air, he saw a splash as Watson entered the water. He also heard Hendrickson laughing and pointing at the splash. Hendrickson also slapped his knees while hopping around in a fit of glee.

Dressler, the remaining Mohawk, stood up and grabbed Hendrickson. They wrestled to the ground and both managed to roll into the water. Everybody was laughing and shouting while the four tried to get out of the water. All of a sudden there was a loud whistle from the top of the hill.

It was the Mister!

The three Mohawks and the one renegade settler, Hendrickson were not allowed to have dessert for supper and had to stand in separate corners until bedtime. Both Mr. and Mrs. Z knew a lot about Byron Hendrickson before he arrived at the New Farm. His deportment had changed for the better during most of that summer but it took two other times when he lost control of his spontaneity. The Zimmerman's played no favorites in giving out punishments but they had a special corner just for Hendrickson.

A thought once awakened does not slumber.

Memory is fragile and fluid. Sifted through layers of time and experience, some edges soften. Others reveal themselves with increased clarity. Sara DeLuca

ADVERSITY by Denis Simonsen

Adversity is no more than a chance
To look back and reflect on happenstance
It's not about what's lost or what's been gained
Or whether there's been sunshine or it's rained

The sum of all you are you freely share
Has not been spent but dwells in hearts that care
The echoes that come calling back are real
The ripples that your words have left you feel

Echoes reach other ears, are just as clear
Ripples reach distant shores as well as near
Past and present intersect and break the spell
Renew your value and self worth as well

Shout into hidden valleys far beyond
Cast words into the still and silent pond

THIS QUIETTIME by Denis Simonsen

This quiet time won't be with us forever
The wind is breathless right before the storm
Shut out the need to scream against the weather
And for a moment listen to the warm

LOOK MOM, NO HANDS by Bob MacKean

It's Saturday, there is no school and I've overslept. I rush to the window looking for my dad's car. It's gone and my heart sinks. I dress and walk outside. A warm, spring morning greets me and dulls some of the disappointment I feel from being left home today. I had hoped my dad would get me up and take me to work with him. He's been stationed at the Naval Air Station in Minneapolis since the end of World War II and would often take me with him on Saturdays.

The distant whine of jet engines gets my attention. A search of the cloudless skies reveals many airplanes flying at different altitudes. Feeling an urge to be at the airport I grab a snack, run outside and climb on my trusty bike to peddle 6 miles to the top of a hill about a quarter-mile from the end of one of the runways. Leaving the bike beside the road, I climb to the crest where I can lay in the soft grass looking at nothing but sky from horizon to horizon.

The Korean conflict dominates the news these days and Wold Chamberlain Field is alive with Navy, Marine and Air Force planes flying endless training missions. An F9F Panther takes off and climbs rapidly right over me and another is close behind. They join up and soar out of sight. In the distance a group of F-80 Shooting Stars move into the landing pattern. This goes on for more than an hour and it's time to head home.

I'm still excited as I climb on my bike and start pedaling down the hill. As I pick up speed I imagine myself as a flight leader of the squadron of Saber jets approaching the runway in formation. With my hands off the handlebars and my arms outstretched I radio the group "follow me boys, were going in fast." and I veer to the left. I have no idea there's a car about to pass me and I turn into its path.

The bicycle shoots out from under me as I fall back onto the car's hood. The screech of tires is all I hear as I bounce off the car and fly across the road into the opposite ditch. I lay still for a moment thinking I must be badly hurt. I move my arms and legs. Everything seems okay. As I start to get up I see a very badly shaken driver walk towards me. I notice that the back of my head really hurts and one shoe is missing. Looking past him I see my twisted bike. The driver appears to be in shock until he sees me get up to go after my shoe. He helps me load the bike into his trunk and offers to drive me home. The color returns to his face as we drive.

My mother comes out of the house as the strange car pulls into the driveway. Not knowing about the accident she seems more concerned about me arriving with a stranger than anything else. After seeing the bike and hearing my story I was hoping that the driver wouldn't leave right away but after my mother got his name and address he was gone. I think she was just glad that I wasn't badly hurt. I got off without even a lecture from my mother but my dad had a lot to say when he got home.

I sure missed having my bike that night on my paper route.

THE TORTOISE AND THE HARE by Denis Simonsen

With apologies to Lewis Carroll and Aesop

The sun was shining on the crowd
And it was hot and dry
No cloud was flying over head
There were no clouds to fly
And this was scarcely odd because
It was the middle of July.

The tortoise said. "It's really grand
That folks would gather here
To watch me win this famous race
To clap and shout and cheer."
The hare replied with much disgust
"They came for the free beer."

"My furry friend," the tortoise said
And flashed a toothless grin
"There is no reason to be miffed
Because I always win
Perhaps it's time to have a talk
Before we both begin."

"For seven years we've raced this race
And seven times you've won
Do you suppose." the rabbit said
"That I could win just one."
"I doubt it." said the tortoise
"I'm having too much fun."

The crowd was getting anxious
For the race to start
For all the folks in Carlton
Had gathered in the park
The famous race would take all day
And finish after dark

"Get on your mark" the mayor cried
The duo soon were gone
The town folks with their picnic lunch
Scattered cross the lawn
For games and naps and friendly talk
They knew the day was long

Meanwhile around the nearest bend
The pair came to a stop
"It seems a shame" the tortoise said
"To carry out this plot"
His furry friend said nothing
Except "It's much too hot".

The day wore on, the food was gone
And as the night grew near
Around the finish line the town folks
Crowded in to cheer
The winner on with a hurrah

And have just one more beer.
Alas, for silence greeted them
No winner appeared there
Where was that steady tortoise
Where was that speedy hare.
"Let's wait until the morning
Then scold that useless pair".

65

There was no joy in Carlton
On every face a frown
Their gold and silver all were gone
When folks returned to town
They shook their heads in silence
Not a penny could be found.

A plane was flying over head
As planes will often do
And in first class the rabbit said.
"They didn't have a clue."
The tortoise raised his glass and said.
"Do you admire the view?"

KING OF THE WILD FRONTIER by Russ Hanson

A friend from my early days passed away in 2010. I first met him December 15th, 1954 when another new friend, Uncle Walt Disney, introduced him to me. His name was Fess Elisha Parker (1924-2010), but I knew him better as Davy Crockett, King of the Wild Frontier. He died last March, but watching a year end memorial list of folks who moved on during the year, I found myself most moved by his death.

I was 5 days into being eight years old, a young man ready for a hero when Disney presented "Davy Crockett, Indian Fighter" on Frontier Land. Disney had started his program, then called "Disneyland," just a few months earlier, showing a mix of cartoons, nature, and adventure episodes. Each week we visited Fantasy Land, Tomorrow Land, Adventure Land or Frontier Land for an hour on Wednesday night (yes, it started Wednesday nights), beginning in October 1954, at 7:30 for an hour (stretching our bedtimes a little).

We had a bought a brand new 17- inch RCA black and white TV earlier in the year. Dad and Mom were convinced it would be educational for us kids. They bought it from Rollie Nelson at the Gamble store in St. Croix Falls. Mr. Edler, the radio repairman from town, came out and installed it. He climbed to the top of our big old farm house and attached a mounting bracket, pipe, and basic 4 rod aluminum antenna high above the house. It looked exactly like two sets of cat whiskers, one behind the other.

"Have to point it towards the SW to get the Twin Cities stations." He ran a flat, two-wire cable down the house, put on a lightning arrester and ran it under the window into the dining room (we ate in the kitchen). He put together the basic stand, four splayed legs under a little table, unpacked the TV, put it on the stand, connected the cable and then pulled off a front panel exposing some of the insides. He plugged it in and tuned to channel 5, then took his screw driver and adjusted the picture (he said he was adjusting a tuning slug coil). He did the same with channels 4 and 11 before putting the panel back on and then calling us all inside. Dad wasn't there, but we kids and mom hovered nearby.

"Right now you get channels 4,5 and 11. I think there is a new channel coming soon on 9 soon. Let's try it out." He showed us the on/off volume control knob. He showed us the channel tuner knob that clicked its way from 2 to 13 (the first thing to wear out). Then he showed us the little door that tipped out to show brightness and contrast and fine tuning pencil sized knobs that we could, but shouldn't adjust.

The very first show we saw was Toby Prin playing church music on a huge organ on channel 4, WCCO. We were already fans of WCCO radio, our good neighbor with Cedric Adams giving us our news however, the idea of TV being filled with church music was pretty worrisome to an 8-year old whose life was pretty much already filled with religion.

Tuning to WTCN -11, we saw a scene of a small boat sailing on a huge lake. Now this was exciting! In the days of black and white photography, black and white TV scenes seemed perfectly normal. Mr. Edler told us a few rich folks in St. Croix and Taylors Falls already had bought color televisions, but very few shows were broadcast in color yet. Life was never the same again; all dates thereafter were measured in BTV and ATV just as history is BC and AD.

When Walt Disney began his Disneyland show in October of that year, we quickly became fans. Mom policed our TV watching, limiting it by time and by shows—no worldly or violent shows for us. Dad rarely watched TV, being in the barn to milk cows in the early morning until 9 at night with meal breaks. He watched nature from the farm, first behind his horses and then from the seat of the tractor and got his news from the barn radio blasting 'CCO to the cows. "I can see the Twins playing ball in my head listening to radio better than the TV shows them live."

Disney immediately passed the suitable for Christian Values test. The closest to sex were the wonderful time-lapse photography of unfolding flowers. Here we saw lions, elephants, tigers and strange places in real life films, television was truly being educational and improving our minds. To us, the Disney cartoons and characters like Mickey, Pluto, Goofy and Donald were all new, since movie theaters, like dances and bars were places of un-Godliness, if not downright iniquity.

Saturday mornings we mostly had to help with the chores on the farm, but sometimes we got to see cartoons or Roy Rogers and Hopalong Cassidy or My Friend Flicka. They were marvelous entertainment, provided upstanding moral role models in the days when the good guys just shot the guns out of the hands of the bad guys and at the end kissed the horse only after being married.

Walt Disney promised us a great adventure at the end of his December 8th program. We would see "Davy Crockett, Indian Fighter" next week in Frontierland. We had no idea who Davy Crocket was, but we figured great, a cowboy show!

We were ready, tuned to WTCN, Channel 11, ABC, broadcast from its powerful transmitter high above the Twin Cities in the Foshay Tower. The show opened with Jiminy Cricket singing "When you wish upon a star, makes no difference who you are.." in his beautiful high voice, while Tinker Bell sprinkled stardust over the screen and Disneyland introduction scenes.

The first of five Crockett shows, as described on the internet by Wikipedia: "Creek Indian Wars: Tennessee wilderness settlers, Davy Crockett and best friend George 'Georgie' Russel volunteer to fight with General Andrew Jackson in the Creek Indian War. After a victorious battle, Crockett and Russel return home over the protestations of their superiors. Returning the next season, the pair find that the pursuing American forces have reached a stalemate chasing the remnant Creek forces through the swamps."
"Georgie Russel is ambushed while scouting for the Indian positions, but Crockett is able to track the Indians back to camp. In exchange for Russel's life, Crockett challenges Red Stick, the Creek's remaining chief, to a tomahawk duel. Crockett emerges victorious but spares the life of Red Stick on condition he will sign the American peace treaty.:

The show introduced us to the "The Ballad of Davy Crockett."
Born on a mountain top in Tennessee
The greenest state in the land of the free
Raised in the woods so's he knew ev'ry tree
Kilt him a b'ar when he was only three
Davy, Davy Crockett, king of the wild frontier

Fought single-handed through many a war
Till the enemy was whipped and peace was in store

And while he was handlin' this risky chore
He made himself a legend forever more
Davy, Davy Crockett, the man who knew no fear

Davy left us the song and some quotes stuck in our heads:
"Grin down a b'ar," "Be sure your right and then go ahead," and of course
"bang goes old Betsey," the name for Davy's long barreled rifle. There
were moral lessons as in the dialog:
Chief Red Stick: "Why you no kill me?"
Davy Crockett: "Maybe because of another law. We have trouble living up
to it, but it ain't bad for red man or white man: thou shall not kill."

Later, when Davy teamed up with Big Mike Fink to fight the River Pirates,
we learned about Davy: "I'm half-horse, half-alligator and a little attached
with snapping turtle. I've got the fastest horse, the prettiest sister, the surest
rifle and the ugliest dog in Texas. My father can lick any man in
Kentucky... and I can lick my father. I can hug a bear too close for comfort
and eat any man alive opposed to Andy Jackson."

We didn't even consider asking our parents to order us a real coon-skin
cap like Davy's; the $1.99 Disney wanted for his genuine (rabbit) coon-
skin cap was way too much. Luckily, our winter caps were fur lined, so
turning them inside out and hanging on a gray squirrel tail, adding a stick
for Old Betsey, and a wood lathe shaped to a point got us ready for meet'n
any b'ar that might come along.

The next day, Davy Crockett was the topic in school amongst those of us
who had TV (not everyone by a long shot). I had the song in my head, and
was singing it over and over. I came home and went to our big old piano,
and sat down seriously for the first time, and picked out the tune after a
little effort. Mom came in and listened as I played it with one finger—and
by summer Marvin and I were sent off to piano lessons to a neighbor,
because I had shown such talent!

Walt had been showing us previews on the TV show about his new
project, Disneyland that was to open in July of 1955 in California. I didn't
get out there to see it until 30 years later, but even then, it was even more
wonderful than Walt had promised. Yep, feels like I lost a real pardner
when Fess Parker passed away this past year.

THREE A.M. EPIPHANY by Denis Simonsen

As fingers of the morning light had traced
Soft circles round your sleep and then were gone
You might have stirred enough, yet not erased
A memory that struggles to live on
From a labyrinth within your inner soul
The flutter of a pair of silken wings,
Thick flaxen hair and eyes as black as coal
A warm and gentle voice that softly sings
Sweet Morpheus has given you a dream
A bit of brightness midst a night of slumber
A vision new or a familiar theme.
The Sandman's done, your mind is full of wonder
Take up a pen and set your spirit free
Combine your dream with your reality.

OCCUPY MOVEMENT ON CAMERA by Walt Fluegel

For generations, novels, paintings, and movies have featured
specific individuals or heroes deeply involved in street protest. These are
our historical understanding of some events. At present, many of the
images we have seen from the Arab Spring were blurry, off kilter, but the
action was understood while a voice-over often told the audience that what
they are seeing cannot be confirmed. We seldom if ever saw a "hero" as
part of that movement.

Now in this country we see the "occupy" movement protests with many
similarities to the Arab Spring. But here there is a big difference. With the
"occupy" movement there is an abundance of recording devices in the
hands of protestors, established known reporters, onlookers and with a few
cops who have wearable video cameras on helmets or on their
uniform. Events unfolding can range from a peaceful gathering morphing
into anarchy. After the cameras have done their work, several questions
are asked by all parties who are recording the event. What actually
happened? Who was involved? What is the message? Was there police
brutality? And from each source there are permutations of how or what to
do with all the video images. Many cameras, many points of view.

Municipalities are confronted with the "occupiers" who wish to "camp
out" overnight in tents erected in plazas or streets. Health reasons are
given which accommodated the overlaying right of free speech and
assembly. However when someone with a thermal recording camera
looked for tent occupiers during the night, many tents were "cold". What
message were we being given? Also, if most of what we see on home TV
is the riotous phases of a protest but a voice-over says this was only a
fraction of the demonstrations, what wins out in the mind's eye, -- the
visual or the voice?

In those city governments that can afford the roughly $200 wearable video
recorder for their police force, cops notice a positive change in behavior of
unruly persons when being told they are being recorded. But once any
police or citizen recording is made, what then? There are many civilian
outlets for the recording, but what about the police recordings? Who will
process and analyze the images? Will the cop be able to explain the
recording once it is handed in to his/her higher rank? If there happens to be

a gray area of interpretation, who makes a final decision? How long must the authorities keep the recordings? Also what is to be done with the recordings held on the shelves? Will any official or civilian be allowed to scrutinize the recordings of many months or years back to find infractions (or lessons) made by the police? Who pays for all this?

I do not have the answers to the above practical questions. Some other philosophical questions I see on the internet are being asked too, such as; was there a mistrust building up throughout the years on all sides of society that we needed to have a camera watching us? (On the streets, offices, stores, schools, transportations, police wearables, and so on.) Is the camera meant to see normal behavior or search for the exception? How many voices or faces must the camera see to get an idea of what is really happening and why? Instead of paintings, novels, and movies that illustrated past history will the camera give a more accurate accounting of today's history when the populous rises up to be heard? Is the camera becoming the equivalent of some mythical deity who sees all and knows all but will not reveal its memory or thoughts unless humans can agree on what the camera sees? Many questions; few if any answers. Click, Walt

THE LIGHTNING STORM WITHIN by Don S. Miller

for Cassidy W.

THE LIGHTNING STORM WITHIN
OH, PLEASE GOD, NOT AGAIN
A LOSS OF CONSCIOUS THOUGHT
CONTROL IS LOST THEN SOUGHT
THIS IS ALL A DREAM
I ONLY WANT TO SCREAM
CAUGHT IN THIS NIGHTMARE
DO DOCTORS EVEN CARE?

THE LIGHTNING STORM WITHIN
OH, PLEASE GOD, NOT AGAIN
I HANG MY HEAD THEN CRY
I'VE OFTEN WONDERED WHY
PUT NOT YOU TRUST IN GOD
SAID THE DOCTOR WHO PLAYS GOD
PUT YOUR TRUST IN DRUGS
I ONLY TRUST IN LOVE

THE LIGHTNING STORM WITHIN
OH, PLEASE GOD, NOT AGAIN
NEITHER WOMAN NOR A MAN
IS FREE FROM SEIZURE'S CHAINS
AN ELECTRICAL REFRAIN
THAT PLAYS MUSIC IN MY BRAIN
CONDUCTED BY A MADMAN
THEN AM I TRULY SANE ?

SOMETHING BETTER by Walt Fluegel

Rimsky Korsakov (RK) at age 20 composed his first symphony. About 20 years later he revised that symphony. How is this connected to photography? Let us consider Ansel Adams. He was a master of the negative film, orchestrating the chemistry, lighting, paper, and timing to produce wonderful prints. Years later Adams made new prints using the same negative. When comparing the older prints with the newer print there were clear differences.

Did Adams deliberately change something in his process to produce the new print? Was the new print better than the first set of prints? Was RKs revised symphony better than the original? Only the observer or listener can tell us, or technical person can point out differences or improvements. I am not an historian so I don't know. Would any one of us, or do any of us photographers go back to one of our original negatives, slides, or downloads and rework the potential image to produce a different print? With digital technology, once I am satisfied with an image it is saved and I know I can make a print any time I want and it will be "the same" every time. (The caveat of course -- all things being equal with the ink, paper, and printer.)

I think it human nature for most people to want to change things "for the better". That is why we now have civilizations and high technology compared to the sheltering caves thousands of years go. Generally, we humans are seldom satisfied with what we have. We keep searching for and working for "something better." As photographers we may do our searching in a photo club or scan a photo magazine for example or follow the advice of some person who we know to be a good photographer. When we have an excellent photo of our own we might still have a twinge of doubt and ask ourselves is it the best I can do? For example, think of that marvelous bird photo, flower photo, scenic, or any image you are particularly fond of and think it the best you have ever made. If we were completely satisfied with the image why do we constantly revisit a bog, flower garden, bird sanctuary or other area to click more images of what we already have? Or are you a "been-there-done-that" type person and seek something completely different.

I understand that Monet had a pond built to grow lilies. He produced over three hundred paintings of those lilies under all conditions. That sounds a lot like photographers in their quest to explore all sorts of unique or novel situations photographing the same objects. Is it "something better" we are looking for or something novel? Whether we are sport, scenic, fashion, industrial, nature or other kind of photographer, I suspect the "something better" or novel for each of us is in harmony with basic techniques and desires to produce good images no matter who holds the camera.

Just as RK and Adams revisited their earlier works there are other artists, photographers and musicians who revisit the work of earlier creators and apply a different technology or look for "something better" that might "improve" the earlier work. Use acrylic paint rather than oil or watercolor. Adapt the musical score for different instruments. Find different filters or a unique lens, or use HDR techniques rather than a single exposure and a naked lens. All these creative variations and more are the product of the human urge to find or create "something better". When we left our comfortable caves and quit drawing on the cave walls, the creative talent was not lost as we became a notch more civilized. When old work is replaced in the list of favorites is it because we have changed or is it because we are always looking for "something better"?   Click, Walt

A well-balanced sense of humor is the pole that adds balance to your steps as you walk the tightrope of life. Wm Arthur Ward

Imagination is everything. It is the preview of life's coming attractions. Albert Einstein

A GREAT FALL by Russ Hanson

Once upon a time, there was a not too young prince, Prince Russ, who liked to build and fix things. One day, he said to his brother, Prince Everett, and his nephew, Prince Bryce, "Let's fix the roof on the sawmill shed on Thursday." After the usual amount of grumpling, Prince Everett and Prince Bryce agreed.

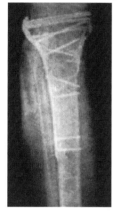

On Thursday, they met at the sawmill shed. "Who will fix the roof?" asked Prince Russ. "Not I," said Prince Everett, "I have to fix the posts." "Not I", said Prince Bryce, "I have to use my tractor to clear the slabs." "Well, then I will," said Prince Russ. And he proceeded to climb to the top of the 100 foot step ladder with a huge board to fix the roof.

Just then a terrible earthquake started shaking the ground. Prince Russ hung on to the ladder with all his might. The ladder swayed left; the ladder swayed right; the ladder jumped up and down. Prince Russ had a great fall. All of Cushing's First Responders and all of St. Croix's doctors couldn't put Prince Russ together again.

A big white ambulance rushed Prince Russ to the World Famous Mayo Clinic where Dr. Sems, cut open his leg on both sides to look at the bone. "Oh, my," said Nurse Johnson. "Bring me my Sears electric drill," ordered Dr. Sems, "and bring me all the metal screws, plates, and hinges that are in the janitors shop." Then Dr. Sems took the bones from the knee to the ankle, which he called the Fibula and Tibia, and started putting them together again. He put in 12 stainless steel screws. He put in two silver spoons. He put in a stainless steel strap that was used for holding a muffler on a car. "Good as new!" he exclaimed after three hours and using up all of his hardware.

"Go home and wait for 100 days and then learn how to walk and everything will be fine, said Dr. Sems. And he was right, except for one thing, Prince Russ had so much iron and steel in his leg, that every night in bed, he rolled and turned around until his leg pointed north like a compass. Although this was a bother at first, Prince Russ never got lost again when he was hunting or camping, because his leg always pointed north!

The following was originally an article I had in the newsletter for the North Metro Photo Club and later It was published in the June 29, 2011 Leader. The words give the images!!

TO BE SPHERICAL by Walt Fluegel

Suppose you were given the topic "Something Spherical" to write about or to photograph. I belong to a camera club and the Northwest Regional Writers. In both clubs we try to hone our skills and present our efforts to members.

For the camera club I "fool around" with things and with the writers I "play around" with words. Let's see what I can do about photography first. "Something spherical". My mind speculates: Suppose I were a sphere? What kind of sphere could I be that is worth photographing and how should I be photographed? There are lots of spheres in this world, including the world we live on -- so let's explore some options.

Frog and fish eggs and the center of hens' eggs are spherical. No way! No photos here because then the yolk would be on me! My muse is egging me on.

Sporting events have lots of spheres so don't pin me down at this point for a photo on bowling. It doesn't strike me as very interesting even though I may have holes in my head as I roll along and crash into things. How about if I were a golf ball? It has cute dimples, and sometimes the ball is embossed with a famous name. But golf balls get smacked across the face by the likes of Tiger Woods or just maybe the usual duffer at the local links. Other balls as in tennis, polo, cricket or even baseball, get smacked by something. Ye gads that's brutal.

In baseball's case, being clubbed on the seams can be mighty tough on my hide. Maybe I can be photographed in the hands of a famous pitcher contemplating a curve ball. Also, I hope I don't get fouled in the process.

In croquet I might be photographed with genteel people. I am in the grass and gently touching some other ball. But then someone steps on my head and pounds me with a large wooden mallet and before I know it I bump my companion and send him rolling along the lawn. I am pounded again and sent through a wire hoop-de-do. Hmm-mm! Is this exciting photography?

Hoops! That reminds me,,,,,, look how a basketball is treated! It's bounced, dribbled, tossed and slam-dunked by powerful hands. I could also be photographed balancing on the end of a finger. Better as a video than a still photo. It makes my head spin just thinking about it. Maybe at this point I should make a note for the writers to go into detail on how I see the players face to face as they make their free throws or as they pass me from one player to another.

From the other extreme, how dull to be a small cannon ball being catapulted into the air by a shot putter and landing with a thud. I think the photographer would concentrate more on the athlete's facial grimace than to take a shot of the shot.

Maybe I would like being a soccer ball's geodesic design, but no photos of this sphere. I don't like being kicked around. And volley ball? With all the ups and downs and sudden spikes only to get sand in my face? ,,, I'll pass. But I can imagine a sports photographer getting a good snap of a player saving a spike while he or she gets sand in the face.

How about if I were a ping-pong ball? Maybe. My light weight allows me to streak and be a blur at 80 to 90 miles an hour just before I bounce from a table. Then WHAM -- I get hit by a sandpaper covered paddle. It makes me spin around, get bounced on a table again and WHAM again! That's rough on my thin skin because that is all I am!

Why not be something solid like colorful marbles? On a Chinese checkers board,,, maybe... but not in the hands of a sticky-fingered kid. Besides, how would anyone make a sticky-fingered kids hand photogenic? And for the writers, how would anyone describe sticky gooey fingers, ugh!

I like the sound of chimes and clangs and bright flashing lights so maybe I would try being snapped in a pinball machine. As a sphere I would travel quite a bit even though I got bounced and flicked around and land in a hole. It's better than being a ball bearing where all you do is go around in circles.

Ahhhh!! Let's look into a crystal ball and pretend in a different direction. Let's see something more genteel, refined, elegant and very alluring. I know what kind of sphere I would like to be! I can dream every man's dream and be lucky enough to be photographed as one pearl resting on a beautiful woman's neck. Hmmm that would be real nice indeed!!

ROOT CANAL by Walt Fluegel

Assignment: Write a story that can fit on a 3 x 5 card.

Dental floss lower jaw. Pain scale 5 left side middle molar. Pain declines in 2 days. Floss again. Pain again, then declines. Pain 2 several weeks only when chewing and flossing. During meal sensation 2 drops to 0. Notice sensitivity when brushing and shaving. Call our dentist in Mpls. "Next week, 9:00 AM Friday". Up at 6 AM. Breakfast, wash-up etc., in car by 7 AM. Winter driving 75 miles. Dentist's X-ray confirms root canal nerve dead and abscessed. Suggests root canal specialist. Prescribes antibiotic. Come home. Get antibiotic. Visit specialist four days later. "Yup, into bone!" Dead nerve, no Novacaine needed. Jaw with rubber mask. Drill, gouge, pressure, scraping, twisting, spraying, suction, call for tools, assistant responds, 3 x-rays. Temp filling after 90 min. Jaw tired. Feel bruised. In 10 days another visit. Sensitivity persists. More drilling, scraping, gouging, pressure. I have permanent filling 90 minutes later. More antibiotic prescribed. "Call if sensitivity persists or gets worse, we may have to do surgery". Ugh! Antibiotic helping. Pain subsides but causing tummy troubles. End antibiotic when all pain gone.

NOVEMBER'S SONG by Denis Simonsen

November's song is bittersweet,
Her gown has fallen 'round her feet.
The rain has washed away her glow,
Her jewelry sparkles in the snow.

A smile is on her weary lips,
For in her tired hands she grips
The seeds that ultimately bring
The promise of another spring.

OUR CHINESE SCROLL by Mary Jacobsen

I don't know who painted our scroll, but I imagine the artist sitting cross-legged on a cushion in front of a low, square table arranging his brushes, his ink stick made of soot and glue, and the inkstone with its indentation for water. I see him twirling the ink stick in the water. The water blackens. When he's satisfied with its concentration, he takes a bamboo-handled brush with fox hairs tapered to a fine point and, holding it straight up and down, dips it into the black ink.

Our artist writes a poem in the ancient art of calligraphy down the right side of the scroll. With the same brush he begins painting fluffy black and gray birds, three in flight and one perched on a crooked branch of a cherry tree. He chooses another brush, with a sheep's hair tip, for the red and pink blossoms on the tree and faint wash of pink for the birds' breasts. The painting comes alive with bird-song and the fragrance of flowers.

Our artist is pleased when he lays down his brush, for in a single work he has united poetry, calligraphy, and painting, considered in China as the Three Perfections, an art form that began over 3000 years ago.

LITTLE PINK CAT by Mary Jacobsen

She guards my jewels, a little pink cat on top of a black lacquered box. Folded polka-dot paws cushion her polka-dot head, and her polka-dot tail curves 'round. She's beautiful, my pink cat with her black polka-dots and purple and orange flowers on her back. Bright green leaves match her bright green eyes that are forever open.

Inside the black lacquer box are earrings with three blue sapphires that swing on three slender gold bars, a pair of intertwined rings of pink, yellow, and white gold, cloisonné turquoise-colored heart earrings with a tiny pearl in the center and another pearl hanging from the heart, a pair of seed pearls in a circle interspersed with tiny gold balls, and my birth stone earrings—garnets in the form of a flower.

I haven't worn any of these jewels since the pink cat took up residence on my lacquer box. I look at those bright green, watchful eyes and I haven't the courage to lift the lid.

DEAR MOTHER by Alice Ford

Dear Mother you gave me a path

When I left it you showed wrath

I never could learn to do math

But I learned not to sass.

You always gave respect, and expected it back.

This is the thing that kept me intact,

Sometimes even blistered my back

You taught me to cook, clean, and mend.

How to hold life, never to bend.

To give. To love, and to lend.

Such a great mother and friend

This I have learned about you.

You're one in a million or two.

God gave me the best he could find,

The greatest of your kind.

In my writing class in college my professor sometimes made notes on how to improve this sentence or that sentence. Occasionally he would write "expand here". As you read the story below, note the possibilities of "expand here".

MY LIPS ARE SEALED   ---- by Walt Fluegel

It was morning. Time to get up. I took care of myself, got dressed, took my pills, and then turned on the computer to check on my e-mails. There was one letter from Mary Jacobsen letting me know what the next assignment was for the writers. The writer's assignment was "My Lips are Sealed." My mind's eye immediately saw a "flighty" blond young woman who had her index finger to her lips. She said in a breathy whisper, "My lips are sealed" and as she did so she rolled her eyes and blinked several times. Then she smiled, turned around and sashayed out of the room.

Now how did this image pop into my mind, and so early in the morning? Perhaps it was a recall from a pseudo spy comedy I saw on a TV program. I got the impression the blond was not a serious person, but then again that may be all part of the act. Play the dumb blond! And be a good spy. So who would believe this blond was a spy! "But wait a minute Walt", I said to myself. It was not too long ago that a famous blond was exposed by a political figure or one of his aids. The woman was a good looker, intelligent, blond but not a dumb blond by any account.

But now what to do about the assignment? No story line came to mind so I did the next best thing I could think of. I checked my computer files of a download I made about a year ago on the origins of sayings and clichés. I thought I might get a good start and go from there. Nope, nothing there. OK, let's Google the expression "My lips are sealed" thinking it may be a famous line in a play or movie. Google popped up with --- Ye Gads, thousands of references, the first batch being references to a 1981 song written by June Widen and Terry Hall and published by MGB Songs. The references looked endless and pretty much the same. There must be more to it than that I thought so I put my writing aside or better yet I left it on the computer desk top because I was getting hungry for breakfast.

I had breakfast, did some chores around the house, got the snail mail after a walk and did some fooling around with my computer art off and on during the day. The writer's topic was out of sight for a whole day and night. But my inner sight began to take hold while I was becoming awake the next morning. The assignment crystallized and intruded itself into what I had to do in terms of daily chores, meal planning and shopping that needed to be done.

I quickly dressed, took my pills, and got to the computer as soon as I could. I ignored thoughts of routine matters. As soon as the computer was fully booted a cascade of thoughts spilled from my fingers --- . Hey Walt, who was that blond talking to, and why was she sealing her lips and why did she leave the room, and why did you use the word "sashayed" instead of a more sensuous term like shapely or perhaps a more common word. "Now we are getting somewhere Walt, --- work on that for a while," I said to myself. "The sealed lips song may be interesting to examine in detail but this other line of thought may be more fruitful." ((Yes I do sometimes talk to myself, not out loud, but I do need to converse with someone with a bit of intelligence!))

OK, so who was she talking to? And why in a breathy whisper? Who told what to whom? What was her name? Because we do not know the message we know nothing of the reason for the lips to be sealed. Was it serious? Was it a call for help or expressing desperation? Was it a socialite or a neighbor telling some gossip about a mutual friend? Was she listening to her daughter who was relating boyfriend troubles? Was it someone who just found out something about her boss from another office worker? Was she really a spy and playing the dumb blond as an act? Well Walt, these could be lines to follow up on. More thoughts came in quick succession.

What kind of blond? Curly? Straight cut? Long hair with waves? That may matter and could be filled in later. And why did she smile as she said "My lips are sealed."? What was going through her mind? Why did she roll her eyes and blink? Oh! And why did she leave the room? What kind of a room was it? Was it at the office? Or home? Or at a party?

I decided to drop the dumb blond spy part, because a good spy is not known to be a spy. No one with a bit of imagination would even think that anyone in particular *is* a spy unless there was some tell-tale evidence. Again, a good spy is not known to be a spy. They blend well into the background much like a grandmother or a favorite uncle or maybe a janitor -- who knows?

But then we have the opposite in James Bond for example. He is not a good spy, because the opposition knows of him almost immediately. He gives a lot of clues that he is a government agent and he has habits that are well known. For example his drinks are stirred not shaken. (Or is it the other way around?) James Bond stories may make interesting movies, with all the seductions and chasing round, explosions, fireballs, destructions, some spying, more seductions, and some run in with his boss "M" or with Money Penny the secretary. All of that makes him a lousy spy. I would not hire him to do serious work.

So you might now ask me why I brought your attention to James Bond. My answer is that James Bond is a diversionary tactic to draw you away from the main topic. So from now on, my lips are sealed.

Solitude provides the fuel for all of life's other requirements.

The death of an old person is like the burning of a library.   E B Sutton (Boyd's dad)

African saying: You will never plough a field if you only turn it over in your mind.

Art is the only way to run away without leaving home.

WHAT ELSE COULD IT BE BUT LOVE – THE KISS by Don S. Miller

What else could it be but love? Notice I didn't say sex, not yet anyway. L-O-V-E, love. It all started with a kiss…

This is about Michelle and me; we grew up together as neighbors and best friends. I mistook her interest in my stallion, Rebel, as the promise of something more and kissed her while we were in the stable. I threw fifteen years of best friendship out the window. Chelle didn't know what to do as our friendship meant everything to her. We were so close and always together; when called for, our names merged into one, "Mitch-shelle."

Our parents did not miss the melodrama unfolding—the awkward silences, the averted glances—and finally had enough. Michelle's dad, Norm Peterson, and my father, Stan Kellog, cornered us both and sent us into the garage to talk out whatever the hell had got into both of us.

"Look, Mitch, Chelle, I don't care how long it takes, what the hell is wrong, you're not just upsetting each other, now the wives say this has got to stop."

"We're going to finish off a six-pack while we watch the first half of the Packer's game. Come on, Norm," and with that he pressed the button on the garage door remote. "I'll open it up at half time and if you still look like two skittish deer on opening day of hunting, I'll close it up again. We'll continue…." With that the door closed and cut off the vision and the sound.

We'd not said a word since that single shared kiss—and the prolonged silence afterward—her shock overshadowed my embarrassment.

We faced each other, her head was uplifted and she looked as though she were about to speak. Tears glistened on her cheek like a knife blade, cutting painlessly downward to stop and collect on her upper lip, only to fall to the floor. As each tear struck the floor, it dropped ice water onto my heart, already aflame, with passion. She turned and began to walk away, and muttered just within hearing,

"Why?"

I followed after her and grabbed her by the shoulders and turned her around to face me. "I've missed you so much," she said, and then she was in my arms, head pillowed on my chest, deep sobs racking her body. As her body convulsed with emotion in my arms, my shirt front became soaked with tears. Then I heard the three words that I'd longed to hear, "I…I love you."

"And I love you. Can I kiss you now?" She nodded, gave me a wink and an incredibly sexy grin.

"Why not?"

When half time rolled around, up came the garage door. We tried our best to look like skittish deer and soon had another half to kiss the afternoon away. Tongues darting and dancing, *how long do you think we can kiss without breathing?*

My heart was jack-hammering in my chest, blood roaring through my ears. I could feel her heart keeping up with mine through her left breast as I pulled her close to me.

The next time the garage door came up, the secret was out. My left arm was wrapped around her and held her nice toned butt cheek, holding her tight at hip level. Her left hand was resting on my chest. We were lip-locked in one fantastic French kiss.

We started speaking the language of love, not sex, that afternoon. It's a mysterious language that doesn't always play fair. We've been speaking it ever since. Sex will be another story for another time but not now, not yet, but soon...

THE PICTURE by Don Miller

His hand paused as it rested on the well-worn doorknob. Sixty years old at least – how many countless thousands of hands had rested on this very spot, grabbed hold, turned it, and entered. How many hundred times had he himself entered through this door. He entered.

Since his father passed away in February, on the 14th of all days, a day devoted to love and lovers, the old house had stayed vacant. His eyes strayed to the painting that his father had purchased down in Mexico when he was but a boy. It was painted on black velvet and the figures on it stuck out and almost made the painting three dimensional. It was that of a matador flinging his cape in front of him as a bull with crazed eyes bore down on him. All, and I mean all the parts of the bull's anatomy were there in living color.

His mother had always sworn that someday she was going to burn that damn picture in the fireplace—strong words for a woman who hadn't sworn but a time or two in her life. His father had bought it mostly for joke value, but insisted that it hang on the wall directly behind the living room sofa. It was the room that the women's church circle met in and where they entertained Pastor Eldert Huxtable one afternoon each week.

 His father would be choking with laughter at the way his mother had carried on. But the pastor, and her friends all knew Nels Forrester and let it slide like water off a duck's back. His mother, Elsie, nearly whipped herself into a "tizzy" anytime she thought of "the picture" as it became known.

Now that his mother and father were both gone, "the picture" was his—to do what he would with it. He'd visited his father's grave and had a one sided discussion with the old timer, his mother was at his father's side, quiet as she mostly had been all their married life. Cancer had taken them both, three years apart.

Well, I have a spot on the wall in my den and I can hang it there. My den is off limits to the kids and Marjorie, my wife so that I can let the creative juices flow, work on, and finish my novels.

Nels Jr. reached up, pulled down the painting, hauled it out and set it in the back seat of his BMW.

ONE WINTER DAY IN TUCSON by Stan Miller

One winter day in Tucson, in a parking lot scene
Evil was manifest in that horrific scene.

A man pulled out his Glock, without taking careful aim,
and many innocent people were killed and/or maimed.

One was a little girl, with brown eyes, bright and keen.
She was only nine years old, her name Christina Taylor Green.

She stepped into eternity, climbed on Jesus' lap,
leaned against his breast, as if to take a nap.

He wrapped his arms around her, and whispered in her ear.
Then with nail-scarred hand, wiped away her tear.

Once again he remembered, what he came to earth for,
for his heart was broken, as it had been many times before.

Then he sang a lullaby, as he rocked his rocking chair,
and held her close, and smiled, as he welcomed her up there.

EXPOSURE by Walt Fluegel

A camera novice gets his pictures back, examines the photos and....
> "OH, OH, too much exposure!"

A doctor sees a person with sever sunburn ...
> "OH,OH, too much exposure!"

A Senator Foghorn taking a bribe and caught on tape by the FBI ....
> "OH, OH, too much exposure!"

Cheating spouse handed photos of unfaithful conduct ....
> "OH, OH, too much exposure!"

Conservative clergyman receives unsolicited catalog of Victoria's Secrets ...
> "OH, OH, too much exposure!"

Teenage nephew of clergyman rescues catalog from waste basket ...
> "OH! OH! OH! OH! Ooooooooooooh!!!!"

IS HUNTER SAFETY CLASS FAILING OUR CHILDREN? by Russ Hanson

A couple of weekends ago, my great niece Karra and great nephew Andrew Hanson went deer hunting for the very first time under the new Wisconsin rules that set aside one weekend for 10-12 year old hunters. They both had just finished Hunter's Safety Training. Although their hunt was successful, it pointed up a serious problem with the Hunter's Safety program that teaches kids how to hunt.

They used their uncle Colby's nice deer hunting stand on our rye fields along the Old River Road. This area is the edge of the farming areas to the east and the sand barrens woods to the left. The woods are a bedroom community for deer who commute nightly to the corn, beans and alfalfa fields on the east side of the River Road, returning each dawn to the oak and jackpine woods and prairie remnants on the west.

They had wonderful luck! Andrew shot a nice 8 point in the morning and Karra a slightly larger 9 point in the evening. My brother Marvin, their grandpa, said "they did everything right—good accurate shots, carefully placed and safely done. The Hunter Safety classes had them prepared for 'harvesting a deer.'"

Harvesting a deer is the euphemism perpetrated by the DNR and sportsmen's clubs for shooting or killing a deer. It is like saying a person "went to eternal rest" when you meant he died. To me it brings up an image of running a huge combine driving through the meadows scooping up deer with a big front reel and spewing out packaged meat and mounted horns on the backside. To "set the harvest" each year the DNR and Sportsmen convene death panels to argue the numbers.

Marvin is an old time hunter and butchers his own deer and did his grandchildren's too. "They charge $70-80 for skinning and cutting up a deer that in the end might only have 40 lbs. of meat. And they keep the hide too!" He can skin and process a deer in just a few hours including running it through his big motorized hamburger grinder. "I know I get my own deer back. At the meat markets they probably mix ones with those that hung out so long they are rotten with yours!"

Well, Everett and I drove over to look at the two deer shot by the first two hunters in the 6th generation of the family to hunt deer in Wisconsin. Great Grandpa Hanson, who came here from Sweden, was thrilled to find that he was allowed to hunt deer—that they didn't all belong to the king or nobles in America. He borrowed his brother-in-law's Civil War Spencer repeater Carbine for his first hunt in the 1870s. Deer herds were increasing rapidly after loggers opened up the great white pine forests and left conditions that favored deer. By the time Dad was a kid in the 1920s, they had mostly disappeared from over hunting.

Andrew and Karra were helping Grandpa Marvin and their dad, Brandon, unload the deer onto the butchering table, having registered it at Stop-a-Sec in Cushing when Ev and I got there.

"It is a little too warm to keep them more than a day before we cut them up," said Marvin. They each had a very nice young buck; 1.5 years estimated Ev, looking at size, condition and teeth.

"Andrew, tell us about shooting your first deer," I encouraged him.

"He came out of the woods onto the edge of the field. I took one shot and he fell down and died, "said Andrew shyly looking at his feet. Uncle Everett and I waited for him to continue.

"Where did you hit him?" I prompted to get him going. "Neck," he replied. And that was it. No more story, no more details; the whole story as far as he was concerned. Everett and I were shocked.

"Didn't they teach you in Hunter's Training that the most important part about shooting a deer is the story? My gosh, you gotta do better than that to be a Hanson! You know, a year from now the meat will be all gone; the rack of horns will be gathering dust on the wall, and all that will be left is your story."

It suddenly occurred to us that the Hunter training folks who harvest deer with rubber gloves and ear protectors and put on a medical mask to gut them out might also have sanitized the "Hunting Story" out of the process too!

Long after Parkinson's disease had robbed my Dad of his ability to hunt, he still participated by telling the stories of hunts of his own and his Dad and Grandpa and Uncles, some more than a century old. If you haven't learned how to tell a good story, by golly, you might as well go to a hunting preserve where they lead an elk out of the pen, place a pail of feed in front of him and take off the rope and let you harvest him.

I don't blame the Hunter Safety people totally. My brother Marvin is sadly lacking in imagination too; sort of a stick to the facts kind of guy; not able to tell a story with texture, flavor, color, embellishment, etc. You know that kind of guy; he likes a perfectly mowed lawn, nails and screws sorted as to size and stored all facing the same direction, and the packages of meat in the freezer all labeled as to type, date, with photos of the individual deer on the wrapping paper.

Now, Everett and I learned from experts. We first watch our Hanson great uncles sit around the parlor at Grandpa's and crack wise. Grandpa got too old to hunt but continued telling stories over Thanksgiving dinner. They knew how to tell stories and passed along ones they heard from their Dad too. They knew that good stories grew a little each year as tidbits from other stories got merged into one. My Dad and his 5 brothers continued the tradition; Uncles Maurice, Lloyd, Chauncey, Glenn, Erv, Ralph, and Alvin, all could spin an engrossing story of a particular hunt (successful or unsuccessful made little difference in the quality of the story).

Anyway, Everett and I have our work cut out for us. There are already 15 members of the Hanson 6th generation aged .5 to 14, all sorely in need of storytelling training. With Hunter's Safety people abdicating this primary function, I guess it is up to us to take over.

I have made an outline for telling a decent deer hunting story. Most of the points are necessary and should be expanded where possible.
1. Selecting the Gun
2. Choosing the hunt site
3. The preparations
4. The stealthy walk to the stand
5. The weather
6. The anticipation and false alarms and the adverse conditions

7. I see the deer
8. Shooting the deer
9. The death scene
10. The drag
11. Statements of false modesty or a moral.

I include my own first kill story as an example. It is very much abbreviated so that it will fit into this column. The story told aloud is what my neighbor George calls a 2-beer tale.

Back in '59, when I was 12, I bought my first deer-hunting license. I had tagged along with Dad and older brother Marvin at times the two previous years and was ready to try it myself. The starting gun for all of us Hansons of my generation was Grandpa's old 38-40 Winchester, fondly nicknamed "the pumpkin slinger." It shot a small rim fire shell that looked like a bloated 22 short. It threw a big chunk of lead a short distance before dropping precipitously. It held 15 shells and had a smooth well-worn lever action. You could lay down a pattern of lead that, with luck, a deer might stumble into.

1959 was one of those years where the Conservation Department was trying to let the deer herd grow a little. Back in the '50s, deer were rare in NW Wisconsin. Every piece of land was heavily pastured by farmers and deer were hunted heavily and never seemed to get any surplus at all. Shooting a deer (bucks only then) was a true achievement requiring a lot of luck and skill. That year, the season north of Hwy 70 was nine days but only from Thanksgiving on around Cushing. Dad decided we would hunt the first day in the Kohler Peet Swamps north of Grantsburg where there was public land.

Saturday dawned bitterly cold with wind and 22 below on the farm. We helped Dad milk the cows early and were finished well before first light. We had long underwear that we wore all winter and rubber buckle boots to wear over our lace up leather shoes. We put on two pairs of underwear; two pairs of wool socks, mittens with liners, our wool dull read caps and a thin red coat over our heaviest old coat. This was before the days of blaze orange, so we were red only from the waist up. Dad took some matches "we will start a fire if we get too cold."

We got out of the green '51 Chev along the road somewhere in woods north of Grantsburg just as dawn was breaking. Cars lined the road. We uncased our guns, walked, the snow squeaking cold, into the woods. We finally found a knoll that seemed to be away from other hunters.

Two hours into the hunt, it was light; we hadn't seen anything, but my toes had long ago abandoned communication with the rest of me. It was really cold! "Get a some dry twigs and birch bark and let's start a fire," Dad finally said. In a few minutes, we had a small fire going; a few minutes later a nice one. Of course, it takes just as long to unthaw your toes as it did to freeze them due to the layers that the heat needs to go through.

Thirty minutes later as we huddled around the fire, a couple of shots rang out nearby. "If a buck comes through, we will have to drop him here or the next hunter will surely get him," Dad counseled as we brought our guns up to alert. Four deer came trotting up through the woods from the direction of the shots. "The front one is a buck," whispered Dad, giving us the OK to open fire.

I think we each shot the first shot simultaneously. The big buck continued forward through brush still 100 yards away. I shot six more times; Marvin 3, and Dad once. The buck fell, but started to get up, so I pumped a couple more shots into him in the head area. We rushed down and found him dead; a very nice 12 point buck. We looked and there were holes in his neck, head; front leg, back leg, hoof and a few miscellaneous nicks. "Well ventilated" joked Dad.

The deer had a bunch of smaller prongs around the base of the big horns that we decided made him an 18 pointer. We drug him up near the fire and Dad showed us how to gut him out (Andrew says you "field dress" a deer now a days).
"We need to tag him," said Dad, "I think we all shot him, so whose tag should we use? I don't want to use mine so I can keep on hunting."

Marvin agreed with Dad, and so they turned to me. "You used the most lead! It can be your first deer."

Years later, we sat around on the porch room where the mounted horns hung at home and each remembered and told the story of the "Big deer from Grantsburg." Each of us had our own version of the story. We can spend at least 10 minutes remembering how cold it was; another 10 minutes on how terrible the gun was; 10 minutes trying to place where the Kohler Peet swamp was; and end up arguing whether the heater in the 51 Chev was any good.

"You know, now-a-days they tell you not to eat venison because of the splinters of lead that might be in it. They say it messes up your brain and lowers your IQ. I bet that Grantsburg buck was full of lead," said Everett staring at the big old set of horns on the wall at Mom's place last week. "Maybe that explains why we put those horns on the bicycle in place of the handlebars the next summer, and why we didn't realize how dangerous it was to drive around with your belly 5 inches from 18 wicked deer prongs," he mused.

Writing is easy: All you do is to sit staring at a blank sheet of paper until drops of blood form on your forehead. Gene Fowler

I try to leave out the parts that people skip.

A professional writer is an amateur who didn't quit.

HUNTERS HIT THE JACKPOT by Bob MacKean

That was the headline on the Milaca newspaper after an ill-fated hunting trip I took with my brother-in-law, Bruce, in the fall of 1962. We were spending the weekend on his uncle's farm to do some pheasant and grouse hunting. Early Saturday morning we headed for the fields with our shotguns and my western style six-shooter in its quick-draw holster with the bullets all around the belt.

Before we got too far the neighbor kid showed up and asked if he cold tag along. He was holding a wimpy looking 20-gauge single shot and we thought we could use him like a bird dog to scare up some game for us.

"Sure come along" we said and would soon regret that decision. He not only flushed 'em , he shot 'em , before we could even raise our guns. Not only that but he was having trouble carrying all the birds and asked if I would carry them for him in my new hunting coat with the game pocket all around the inside. I made another bad decision, I said yes.

When a big rooster jumped up in front of us, Bruce and I were ready, we thought, but before we could get a shot off, boom the little twerp downed another one. I told him I wasn't going to lug around anymore of his birds and he would have to take back the ones he had already shot. This sent him home and we thought now that we could get some hunting in. He must have put a hex on us before he left because every field we tried came up empty. On the way back,, we came across a dilapidated old farm that his uncle had bought to expand his cropland. The saggy looking barn was empty except for a flock of pigeons roosting in the rafters. Desperate to shoot any kind of bird we fired at them but all we ended up doing was ventilating the roof.

Then we approached the house. Bruce went around the outside, I wanted to see the inside. As I entered I imagined there were bad guys hiding around each corner. I drew my pistol and shot up some door frames to see the wood splinter like in the old westerns. I looked into the living room through the kitchen door and saw a Zerex can on the floor. It looked like a good target, but before I could put a couple of holes in it, Bruce poked his shotgun through the window and said "Stand back."

I backed up a step and waited until he shot. At first, the blast, sounded loud like I expected but it didn't stop. The roar continued and I felt myself being lifted and floating across the kitchen. I landed in a corner under a lot of lathe and plaster and watched a large staircase break off the wall and land at my feet. I huddled until everything quit falling then checked myself for injuries. My head hurt and my ears were ringing but otherwise I was ok. I crawled across the debris to the doorway I had been standing in. I could barely get through it, the walls had moved and most of the living room ceiling was on the floor. Looking to my left I noticed the window where I had last seen Bruce. I climbed through and onto the porch. I yelled for Bruce and noticed movement in the tall grass about thirty feet away. I ran to him yelling, "What happened, are you ok?"

He asked me what happened and I said there must have been a gas tank behind the house. As he crawled around looking for his gun I noticed the blood running down the sides of his head. Not knowing where it was coming from I told him to hold his head to stop the bleeding, but it didn't help.

I said "We have to get back to the farm. You need a doctor."

As we started walking the half mile the blood looked worse so I said, "Let's run you're losing blood too fast, we got to get there quick."

Before we got to the house, Bruce said his mother was going to faint if she saw all the blood. He was soaked to the waist, and I suggested we go into the milk cooling room next to the barn and wash him off a bit, but before we could get there his mom and aunt saw us and rushed to help. His uncle was still in the fields so I got my car and we loaded Bruce onto the front seat with towels wrapped around him.

The ten mile trip to the Milaca Hospital probably took less than ten minutes. He was very week when we got there but able to walk inside. They put him in a treatment room right away and checked me out in the hallway. Besides the constant ringing in my ears, I just had a bump on the head. I sat there listening to the sound of glass chunks being dropped into a metal pan as they worked on Bruce.

Meanwhile his uncle had been on a tractor working in a field when he heard the explosion. He knew exactly what happened. The dynamite he had been suing to blow up old tree stumps around the house had been put in a Zerex can when it started raining , then placed inside the old house to keep it dry till he could come back. He told us this when he came to the hospital. Ten sticks of really good stuff sure did a number on that house.

Bruce stayed in the hospital for a couple of days after they replaced his blood and sewed up a bad cut behind his ear where a piece of glass from the window he had shot through went right through his ear. Having his gun tight against his face when he shot had saved his eyes. I went back to the blast site the next morning to take pictures and look for Bruce's gun. Naturally this was a topic of conversation for years to come and Bruce and I had a good laugh over the newspaper headline but we never hunted together again.

ODE TO THE IRON RANGE by Don S. Miller

The massive docks and piers are silent now where iron ore carriers had come heavily laden and had delivered millions of tons of iron ore. In the twenty-first century we forget that iron ore had been king three decades ago, and that ships had gambled, defied the odds, and had tempted fate as they traversed the treacherous, hellish waves, and sometimes had lost the wager. In shipwrecks, tens of thousands of tons of Taconite ore accompanied men to their frigid watery tombs on the bottom of Gitchee Gumi, Ojibwe for Great Freshwater Sea—Lake Superior. In sparsely populated Hickerson County, Wisconsin, the death clutch of winter holds long, it spares nothing and no one. Atherton, Wisconsin is dead Small Town, America, located within a snowball's throw of the shores of Superior, the Icy Lady—the Frozen Mother—whose lingering caresses cause death from hypothermia, and the frozen dead never rise from the depths of her frigid watery womb.

BLIND MAN'S BLUFF By Don S. Miller

A tall man carried a thick bulbous-headed cudgel in front of him. Hooligans crept up behind him and prepared to beat the tall man senseless with his own stick. He whirled about, his gaze not fixed on any one, but the whole of them as a group. One by one they came at him, his mind not focused on the movement but the sound and struck them with unfailing accuracy and laid his would-be-attackers low before him. He turned slowly and strode down the street and stopped in front of a doorway.

"Good morning, Reverend Downing," said the ladies of ill commerce.

Reverend Downing sniffed inward, noting the aromatic sexual elixir of their trade and heard as silk slid over naked bodies—these were high class whores who dared address a man of God in public view, "Good morning my dear sweet beautiful ladies," he sniffed inward again and they giggled like little girls.

He adjusted his dark eyeglasses, entered the doorway, the sign above it read Chapel Hill School for the Blind, where he was teacher.

The English language has far more lives than cat. People have been murdering it for years. Farmers' Almanac

A good storyteller is a person who has a very good memory and hopes that other people haven't. Bernice Abrahamzon

If it weren't for our presumptuous desire to learn, humanity would have the same aspirations as a herd of cows. C. O'Brien (Popular Science Jan '06)

TO GRAMMATICALLY WRITE RITE by Russ Hanson

"When I use a word," Humpty Dumpty said in rather a scornful tone, "it means what I choose it to mean, neither more nor less."
"The question is," said Alice, "whether you CAN make words mean so many different things."
"The question is", said Humpty Dumpty, "which is to be master – that's all."
From Alice in Wonderland by Lewis Carroll

Having a weekly newspaper column for the past seven years, we have had some criticism of our writing style, punctuation, word usage, spelling and grammar. It is time to respond to the criticisms and review grammar rules so we all can learn and improve in the future.

Doc Squirt (Roy Hennings), a Cushing native who wrote for many newspapers from 1900 to his death in 1943, was often taken to task by his editors for his lack of punctuation. He solved it by sending the editors a typewritten page filled with commas, periods, colons, semicolons, question marks and exclamation marks with the instructions to "feel free to sprinkle them throughout his columns."

I am more like Mr. Dumpty in that I have never, ever, ever, been intimidated, by grammar, and know who is the master! So without farther adieu, here are some lessons.

Utilize ostentatious language: Never use a simple word when you can think of a big one. Thusly, utilize replaces use; canine for dog; automobile for car, etc. I especially like the signs on Hwy 87 designating Evergreen Avenue, the route to horsie camp as the "Equestrian" area.

Create interest with verb conjugations: You have numerous alternatives. I shall be giving examples in the first person (I), but remember you have the "I/me/my" "he/she/thee/thy/thine", "we/they/them", and of course the "ye,you,thou" singular/plural and objective, subjective and possessive too. If you want to be a good writer, you should practice each variation that follows in a sentence. Sometimes you can change the mood of a story by switching from the past/present/future indicative, subjunctive or conjunctive mood to another, especially in your dependent clauses.

Use the right conjugations: The infinitive verb "to write" conjugates thusly:

the present basic	I write
the present progressive	I am writing
the present perfect	I have written
the present progressive	I have been writing
the past basic	I wrote
the past progressive	I was writing
the past perfect	I had written
the past perfect progressive	I shall/will have written
the future basic	I shall/will write
the future progressive	I shall/will be writing
the future perfect	I shall/will have written
the future perfect progressive	I shall/will have been writing
the intensive present	I do write
the intensive past	I did write
the habitual past	I used to write
the "shall future"	I shall write
the "going-to future"	I am going to write
the "future in the past"	I was going to write
the conditional	I would write
the perfect conditional	I would have written
the subjunctive,	If I be writing, if I were writing.

Non-standard usage: I be writing, I done rote, I have wrotten, I writed it, I writ it, and Dudley do write.

I use Microsoft Word to write my columns. Word has a basic grammar checking tool built in that along with spell check that fixes half of my problems and creates 25% new ones by sowing doubt.

Punctuation marks: The seasoning in writing. They try to tell the reader how the writer felt and more importantly, the pauses to take a breath if one is moving his lips while reading.

Punctuation used by most of us includes the period, the comma, the apostrophe and the exclamation mark. Adventurous authors sprinkle semicolons: very brave authors will try a colon on special occasions: Her colon was cleansed before the x-ray.

Emoticons: Punctuation marks are rapidly changing with the introduction of emoticons. Exclamation can be represented by the "!" mark, but how do you indicate sadness without a sad faced emoticon :-(or a smile :-). Sadly, when I emoticonize my writing, the Leader newspaper, in translating from the PC to MAC computers, loses them and what you see are ? marks in the printed text.

Quotation marks. "Put commas, exclamation marks and periods inside the quotation marks!" Question marks rarely go outside. "You too, Brutus?" Did Caesar say "You too, Brutus"? The second example has a quotation within a question. If you always punctuate inside quotes you will be 90% correct, and the rest of the time, no one will notice anyway.

Who's on First: the correct use of "who," "whom," "who's," "hoo," "hoose,"
"Hoose" is only used in "hoose gow" a euphemism for the slammer.
"Who is" can be shortened to who's. "Who's going to town."
Whose: "Whose shoes are those?"
Whom: you should be able to get through life without using this word.
"To whom do I owe my knowledge of grammar?" is better replaced by, "Who taught me grammar?" If the answer is him, the question uses whom; if the answer is he, then the question is who.
Who loves you baby? He does! Whom do you love? Him! "Whom" is popular amongst and betwixt those whose sign is Antiquarius.

An owl says "hoo hoo" when commenting on the world in general. An owl who says "who? who?" is likely a philosopher. The owl in my back yard says "Who? Who? Who? Hoo, hooooooooer" asking and answering herself as do most females. Generally most people don't give a hoot about this.

Contractions: Shortening words by replacing letters with an apostrophe; gov't, can't, they're, she'll, o'clock, it's and the creative I'd've . Gov'r Palin speaks in contractions as in "I'm runnin' for pres'dent to be savin' us from death panels."

Possessive Apostrophes: Darla's womb's muscle's fiber's cell's nucleus' DNA strands were punctuated by contractions. Ownership is shown by the addition of the "apostrophe s" except in some cases where we already have enough s's and just add the apostrophe at the end—Russ' books.

To Boldly Split Infinitives: An infinitive is a verb preceded by the word "to." To run, to walk, to go, to write, to talk or to split. Grammar rules say don't break them up. It's best never to unintentionally split infinitives (unless you want to really emphasize something). I am willing to strongly predict writers will obsolete this rule at the World Grammar Society meeting in Helsinki in 2015.

"Remember Ramses, it's horse before cow except after sow"

Passive voice: Using was, were as part of your verb with the intention of putting your readers to sleep. Examples include: "Mistakes were made" instead of "I made mistakes." "Margo was talking in a passive voice after having Botox injected into her vocal cords last week" instead of "Margo speaks impassively after the Botox shot."

Adjectives and Adverbs: Words that add color to your sentence. I shot a deer. Shot is a verb, if you color it, you use adverbs. Rapidly, boldly and colorfully, I shot carefully and accurately at the huge brown hungry deer. The "ly" adverbs describe the verb "shot" with "huge, brown, and hungry" adjectives describing the noun deer. Adjectives and adverbs are necessary to make things interesting and are especially useful if you are paid for writing by the word.

Homophones To, Too, Two: Use two for 2, too if you mean also or too much and the rest of the time use to. The two boys were too used to having cake and ice cream too, to be satisfied with less. With society becoming more tolerant, homophonobia has pretty much disappeared.

Euphemism: replacing a strong word with a weaker one. I shot a deer becomes I harvested a deer. The deer died becomes the deer went to heaven. People who criticize my grammar are anal retentives becomes people who criticize my grammar need a hobby.

If you want more grammar lessons, please send a note and we will be glad to take on "their, there, they're", "lie, lye, lay, lied, laid", "buy, by, bye", "sit sat, set, sated, and besotted" and protractions, retractions, subtractions, abstractions, refractions, extractions, attractions, and transactions.

"Nostalgia is like a grammar lesson: You find the present tense and the past perfect" said Robert Orben.

IN THE FLORAL SHOP by Walt Fluegel

"Hi! Alan, how goes it?"

"Not bad, Nick, more interesting this time."

Alan was a mystery shopper for a small consumer research company
owned by Andrew 'Nick' Nickerson. Alan handed Nick a work sheet
form and a small cassette from a miniature tape recorder. Most mystery
shoppers often left "Other comments" at the end of the form blank. Alan
always had something included. That is why Alan was chosen for this
particular type of job. It was important to Nick to get a first or lasting
impression of shopping experience. First impressions by customers were
vital, because first impressions were important to Nick's clients.

"Here is my work sheet, Nick. You decide. Looks like an interesting
prospect to me. Better than the Champion stores."

"Yeah...I know Alan. ....but somebody has to do it." Nick began to read
Alan's report on Arleen's Floral and Gift Store with an occasional
"interesting" or "Hmmmm" "OK...OK...OK," as he went down the list of
responses on the standard form.

Each of Nick's agents, like Alan, acted as if they were customers in every
way except after they shopped and left the store, they wrote down on a
form their own experiences, the stores environment, the clerks handling of
each customer and other bits of information vital for Nick's clients, who
were store or franchise owners.

In this case Nick wanted to acquire more clients because more clients
meant he could increase his business and move out of his basement home
office into better accommodations.

Store owners wanted to know about customer relations. Were the clerks on
their best behavior even if the owner was not in the store? Is it sort of like
spying, but more than that? The mystery shopper was essentially invisible
to any clerk of a store, a usual customer, no one in particular, someone
who blended into the woodwork, someone the clerk had to satisfy and
make happy to have been in the store. The shopper had to be like an

ordinary person, no one special, someone with a blank face maybe, no one who would provoke a clerk. So Nick's clients also wanted to know ordinary customer's experience when they come into a store even if they, the owner, were in the store themselves. Maybe the clerks were on their best behavior only if the owner was in the store. After all, the object is to keep customers coming back as often as possible. The client can handle his or her own advertising to lure in customers, but once in the store, the customer's impression becomes vital. Did they come in because of the advertising, the product, a good first impression, or the feel of the store? What might be the reason they came back? Anything Nick could do to help his clients meant that they would come back to him and he, too, could stay in business.

After Nick read Alan's report about Arleen's Floral and Gift Store, Nick gave Alan the usual monthly Champion assignment. The assignment was now routine. Alan had been a mystery shopper for almost a year. He was getting a bit weary of driving the same route every month. He had three different routes per month. He was given the list of clients to evaluate, a ten to twenty dollar item to buy, forms to fill out, and the time which the overall assignment had to be completed. When he finished, he handed in reports, accounted for the items he purchased, got reimbursed, and received a check for the designated mileage of the route, and another check for "services rendered".

Each of Nick's shoppers was legally an independent freelance agent. They were not employees. So Alan's latest assignment yesterday to Arleen's Floral and Gift Store was a welcome relief. He waited for Nick's reply.

Alan's assignment was to purchase a dried plant arrangement to be delivered within a week's time, so, *"It has to be now"* Alan remembered Nick saying yesterday. So that afternoon Alan went to the store. As he entered, he reached into his pants pocket and clicked on his stop watch then reached into his breast pocket to click on a very sensitive, voice activated, miniature tape recorder.

The store was very attractive outside, neat inside but a bit overstocked in parts, well lit, soft music in the background, and two clerks busy with customers. Three scattered customers were examining different items. Because the clerks were busy, this gave Alan time to absorb the surroundings and commit it to memory. A few moments later as he came close to one of the clerks with her customer, she excused herself to the customer, and directed her attention to Alan for a moment and said, "Someone will be with you shortly."

"That's OK, I'll just look around." Alan replied.

He noticed she was wearing a shiny brass identification badge with the name FRANCIS inscribed in an attractive font more elegant than the badges seen on Champion Auto employees. He went past the counter where live flowers were made into arrangements. Behind that counter he saw limp flowers and greenery scattered on the floor and trampled upon. The waste bin was full and overflowing. The counter needed cleaning. That part of the store could have been neater he thought. He turned around when he heard a pleasant voice say. "May I help you?"

The clerk was a middle age person, a bit hefty, wore glasses with sparkles on the rim, and had salt and pepper hair. She wore a black business type dress jacket and skirt. She did not have a badge. Alan asked her if she could make up a dried flower arrangement to be delivered. Yes she could, but she suggested it might help if he could look in a catalog to pick a type because each one was never exactly the same as the next. The clerk also showed him some raw materials to be used. That was fine with him so they both looked at photographs from a small catalog. Alan made his choice. The clerk said she knows a lady who could do a fine job and that the delivery could be made by the end of the week. The clerk and he had good rapport with each other. There was no difficulty with the delivery time or destination, and Alan paid the bill in cash and got his receipt.

When he opened the door to leave the store, he reached into his breast pocket to switch off the small tape recorder. He also clicked off the stop watch. As he walked to his car in the parking lot around back he noticed the store was one of several sharing the lot, and the lot needed maintenance on the far end.

The first thing he did when he got into his car was to write down the name of the first clerk who noticed him as he came into the store. This was important, because Allen had one odd quirk of memory; people's

114

names. He was getting better at it each time but when there was no name it was easy to report that no name tag was present. He dutifully recorded the amount of time spent in the store and then clicked the stop watch back to zero. The rest of the report seemed routine even with this new store.

Two days later he took the northern rout of Champion Auto stores, shopped the eight stores and was back in time for supper. The next day he had to make several phone calls to other Champion Auto stores asking each one if they had such-and-such a gizmo for a particular car and its cost. It was all part of the Champion Auto mystery shopping Nick had in his contract with this national franchise. It was routine and for each store called, a form had to be filled out. So three days after Allen shopped at Arleen's Floral and Gift Store and the Champion stores, he went back to Nick's office to get the usual reimbursement and new assignment.

"Hi Alan, how goes it?" Nick asked as usual.
"Oh, routine so far." Alan responded.

"Thanks to you we have a new client!" Nick said with a grin.

"What did I do so differently, and who is the client?"

"Arleen's Floral and Gift."

"That was a nice place. Did you get the flowers I ordered for you?"

Nick didn't answer but said, "Let me tell you something good. Here, sit down." Nick gestured toward the chair next to his desk. "I waited until yesterday and went to the store with your report. The lady you worked with was the boss herself, imagine that." Nick reached over to Alan and touched him on the arm as he continued to talk.

"She was very impressed with it and did not mind that you called her hefty, it was better than being called 'fat'." With that Nick made a hearty laugh and put his cigarette in the ash tray. "She thought you had good powers of observation the way you described her glasses, and the store ambiance." Alan said something that it came natural to make descriptions, because he did a lot of that when he worked in the lab in his old profession as a research biologist. Nick continued with another laugh and a chuckle.

115

"What really got to her was that she herself always insisted that her employees in her three other stores wear their badges, and that one day she forgot to pin hers on to her jacket. I think that little observation got us this new client."

"I think too, Allen, that you may have been discovered. When she read the report she remembered only one customer who ordered a dried flower arrangement, paid in cash rather than credit card on the very day when she did not have her badge on." Nick again touched Alan's arm. "Talk about putting several things together, imagine that! When Mrs. Owens, that is her name, thought about it, she began to describe you in great detail."

"I think I know what that means." Alan said, then added; "What about the other stores?"

"Can't risk it I'm afraid. She goes to the other stores on a random basis to help out or relieve staff now and then. You would be spotted right away. You will no longer be a mystery shopper to her."

Well at least for almost an hour Alan was truly invisible as a regular customer, and he did enjoy the adventure. In the next few days he was back to the Champion stores hoping Nick could find a different assignment.

BILLY SPICCOLI'S BASEBALL by Michael Veith

My grandson Louis came into my study the other day, decked out from head to toe in his little league baseball uniform. A bright blue hat sat perched on his head, the number eleven adorned his chest, and his baseball glove was securely fitted to his left hand. A birthday present from earlier in the summer, the glove had been meticulously cared for, softened with saddle soap and rubbed with oil on a regular basis. With an air of professionalism one might expect from a major league team captain, he leaned against my desk and said, "Whaddaya say we go outside and toss a ball around?" I smiled, recognizing my own son's nine-year-old voice and said, "Good idea, chief, perfect day for it."

I haven't owned a baseball glove for many years so I squared off, bare handed, across the back yard and stooped down to take a pitch. The throw was right in the strike zone and I caught it like a pro. Before I could toss it back I couldn't help noticing that the ball was worn almost beyond belief. Once white, the baseball was stained almost black, the stitching was nearly nonexistent and the leather skin hung loose in several places. Louis noticed me examining the ball and gave me a sheepish look. "It's kinda worn out, Grandpa," he said. "You don't have a better one do you?"

It occurred to me in that moment that children never ask easy questions. Although a simple yes or no would have been sufficient, Louis had asked me the one question that I could not find an answer to. "Why don't you set up some bases," I finally said. "I'll go inside and look around."

Upstairs in my study I reached up to the top bookshelf and took down a small acrylic box. Inside, a plain, new looking baseball sat upon a small pedestal. A thin layer of dust had settled on the top pane of the box. I wiped it clean with a handkerchief, opened the back panel and held the ball in my hand for the first time in over ten years. In the back of my mind, I could still hear the roar of the crowd as I recalled the first time I touched that ball.

It was 1946, the war was over and the world seemed ready for a brighter future. I was eleven years old that summer, and Billy Spiccoli was twelve. We lived in the Bronx, only two blocks apart and had been the best of friends since the first grade. During the war years, we had become accustomed to scrimping and saving every little thing that had value, donating much of it to various collection sites to support the men overseas.

Now, as if a spell had been lifted, people began casting off carelessly all those things that had once seemed so priceless. Metal cans, glass bottles, wooden crates and rubber tires were found in abundance, easy pickings for two enterprising boys. We spent our summer days loading our wagons with valuables of every sort and trading them for pennies and nickels at grocery stores, lumber yards and scrap dealers. The daily effort kept our pockets jingling with loose change and we were never in short supply of gumdrops and root beer barrels. Candy, in its many forms, remained a high priority but we always saved enough to go downtown and see the Yankees play once a week.

The second Saturday of July, Billy and I counted our money and rode the trolley to Yankee stadium. In a rare and unexpected turn of luck, we managed to get tickets on the first deck, right above the Yankee's dugout. We always brought our baseball gloves to the games hoping for a chance to grab a foul ball or maybe even a home run, but our usual upper deck tickets offered few opportunities and even fewer near misses. With high expectations, we found our lucky seats and settled in for the game.

Foul balls were abundant that day, but there were plenty of boys in the stadium, all too eager to chase after them, and our hopes grew dim as the ninth inning approached. The score was tied three to three when Joe DiMaggio stepped up to the plate. He swung twice for two strikes and the crowd was on its feet when the third pitch came across the plate. The crack of the bat was deafening and Billy and I held our breath in anticipation. It was another foul ball. It seemed to fly a mile in the air, but when it started back down, we both knew it was going to be a close call. The foul ball headed straight for Billy and I saw him reach his glove high into the air.

Thinking back, it seemed as though I watched that ball for an eternity as it nicked the top of Billy's glove and smacked down on the empty seat next to him. It took a wild bounce high into the air and started back down on my side. I reached out my glove at the last second and made the catch. I stared in amazement at my glove, almost unable to believe what was there. A foul ball hit by Joe DiMaggio himself, the finest thing a boy could possibly own. The spell was broken when I turned and looked at Billy. His face was red and he seemed to be on the verge of tears.

"It's my ball," Billy said. "He hit it to me, it was on my side."

"You missed it," I replied angrily. "It bounced fair and square and I caught it." I simply couldn't believe that Billy would try to take my prize. "Fair and square," I said again. "It's my ball and I'm keeping it." I turned and stormed out of the stadium. The game was over, but I didn't know who won and I didn't care if Billy was coming with me or not. Billy didn't speak to me for the rest of the summer. Although he lived right down the street, I rarely saw him and we spent our time playing in different neighborhoods.

In the fall of that year, my father was offered a job at the Ford plant in Michigan. With only two weeks' notice, we packed our things and prepared to make the move across the country. On the morning of moving day, I stood in the empty living room with my father, feeling frightened and uncertain of what my life would be like in a strange new place.

"I know you said goodbye to most of your friends," my father said, "but I think you should go and talk to Billy Spiccoli."

"Billy hates me," I replied, "all because of a stupid ball."

"Well, if it's just a stupid ball, why don't you go give it to him. A baseball isn't worth a friend, Walter. In a few hours, we're going to drive away and you'll never have another chance to make up with him."

I stomped and brooded around the empty house for a while, but eventually I opened my suitcase and took out the baseball. At length, I decided my father was probably right. I never used the ball, and Billy had been my best friend for years. I swallowed my pride, walked to Billy's house and rang the bell. I could still see anger on Billy's face when he came to the door, but I stood my ground and held out the baseball. "He hit it on your side," I said, "It's your ball."

In the wink of an eye, Billy and I were best friends again. We both felt sorry about the weeks lost being angry at each other and promised to stay

119

friends. We talked as long as we could about Michigan and the new school year and the Yankees, but all too soon I had to leave. I wrote down my new address, shook Billy's hand and walked home.

I never saw Billy again or spoke to him in person, but our lives were destined to be linked in a bond of friendship that transcended time and distance. The sort of friendship that most people are lucky to have once in a lifetime. My family settled into a new life in Michigan, with jobs, schools and new friends taking up most of our time. I often thought about sending a letter to Billy, but I could never seem to find the time.

The week before Christmas, the postman made his daily delivery, and among the cards and letters I found a package with my name on it. I recognized the handwriting and I knew it was from Billy. I wanted to open it right away, but my mother said it was a Christmas present and insisted that I put it under the tree. Christmas was still a week away, so I quickly addressed a card to Billy and put it in the mail.

On Christmas morning I sat in front of the tree with my sister and gazed at the wonderful pile of presents. I reached for Billy's package first, and tore it open. Inside, I found the baseball with a note. "You caught it fair and square," it said. "It's your ball." I promptly put the ball on a shelf in my room and forgot about it for almost a year. I sent a birthday card to Billy that summer, but I never got around to writing a letter, and in the early part of December, the baseball on my shelf began nagging at me. I couldn't help noticing it every time I walked in the room and after two weeks I just knew I had to do something about it. I found a box in the storage closet and put the baseball in it along with a note. "He hit it on your side, it's your ball." I addressed the package to Billy and paid the postage with my own money.

For fifty-two years Billy and I sent that ball back and forth across the country. Always at Christmas and always with the same note. We both moved several times, but we kept up with the address changes and never missed a year. I had the ball on the odd years and Billy had it on the even. Occasionally, we exchanged short letters, but always, there was the baseball.

In 1998, I was surprised to find a package in the mail in late November. I opened it and found the baseball inside with a note in a hand I didn't recognize. "Dearest Walter," it said. "Bill didn't want you to know, but he has been fighting cancer for the last three years. He asked me to send this to you and he said, 'Tell him he can't send it where I'm going, so just keep the darn thing. He caught it fair and square.' He found his peace with God, Walter, and he'll be going home any day now. He loves you like a brother and I will miss the stories he used to tell about the two of you. All my love, Marlene."

I set the baseball on my kitchen table, put on my hat and coat and walked outside behind the house, still in my slippers. I sat down on the edge of the woodpile, ankle deep in snow and wept until my beard was frozen with tears. I found my own peace with God that Christmas and I know I will cherish Billy Spiccoli's baseball as long as I live.

I looked out the window of my study and saw that Louis had found some scraps of cardboard and assembled a makeshift diamond. I walked outside with Billy's baseball in my hand, took a spot on the pitcher's mound and threw out the first pitch of the game. We played catch and Louis ran the bases for over an hour until my wife insisted that we come in for supper. As I placed the ball back inside its box, I noticed that it was now adorned with several bright green grass stains. Somehow, I don't think Billy would mind.

Carefully, I grasp the stem of the cherry, lay its red crispness into my mouth and bite down. The juicy berry spills its liquid onto my tongue, spreading the cool, sweet juice down my throat. Gently, I pick up the slim, long-handled spoon, savoring the moment when I dip into the edge of the whipped cream, gently push the spoon down through the pecans and into the rich, smooth hot chocolate, through the butterscotch and into a small bit of ice cream. Now, I lift the spoon carefully, trying not to spill the concoction down the outside of the glass. Slowly and deliberately the spoon goes into my mouth. There is a noticeable peak for each flavor and texture--the fluffiness and oiliness of whipped cream, the cool creaminess of ice cream, the thick coating of chocolate on the tongue, the slick sweet caramel of butterscotch, and the salty, crunchy, oily flavor of pecans. It is absolutely delicious! Over and over I repeat these rituals, watching the ingredients blending into each other until the glass is completely empty and the spoon tinkles in the bottom of the glass.

What a delightful experience. And what a wonderful memory!

TRIPLE LIFE by Michael Veith

Set down and make yourself comfortable, Joe, no need to be in a hurry now. You ain't the first man I seen come through that door, but I reckon you'll be purt' near the las'. No reason for the good Lor' to keep me on this earth much longer than another short spell, least as near as I can tell. This side here is mine, and that side there is yours, but I done spent enough time on both sides to be purty much at ease either way. I reckon I'll get to know you soon enough, Joe, Lor' knows I always do, so make yourself at home.

I done wrong, Joe, and I can't deny it, that's why I'm here. I wouldn't a done wrong if I'd a known how my life would be, but I done wrong and there ain't no takin' it back now. I reckon there's a good many ways for a man to live his life that's a sight better than the way I've lived mine, but thinkin' on back, it ain't a been all that bad. I eat and sleep well enough and I've made a few fren's now and then, though most of 'em is long gone now. Ever' now and then I gets to have a little time outdoors, but it don't seem the same anymore. I sure do wish I could spen' just one day a sittin' in the warm sun. Seems to me that the sun just don't have any warmth to it by the time it get all the way in here.

I learned my writin' along the way and I practice it ever' time I can get a piece of paper and a stub of pencil. Nowadays I can write near ever' word I can say. Most times I can read 'em too, not always, but most times. I can recite nine poems from memory, one of 'em is considerable long 'bout a sailin' ship. I won't recite 'em now, though, there'll be time enough for poetry, that's for sure. I reckon I spent enough time a makin' shoes and caskets to say I done earned an honest livin' these past sixty one year.

'Bout the only time things gets awful tough is when winter set in real good and a body just stay col' all the time.

It's long 'bout the coldest part of winter, Joe, when things seem just as low as they can be, that I finds me a little piece of happiness. The ladies guild over at St. Mary's gets together and send a little somethin' to me and the fellas for Christmas. Sometimes it's just a card or a letter but sometimes a little gif' along with. One year I got a handkerchief, white as snow, with my name on it in stichin' so fine you couldn't tell one from the next. Don't have it no more though. Ten year ago, my fren' he took ill and died on New Years day. Only thing he ever wanted was to be buried with somethin' nice. Well, I reckon that handkerchief was just 'bout the nicest thing I ever did own, so I sent it off to be buried with him.

Took me near on five year to learn to write "thank you" to those ladies. Lor' knows I done tried, but the words just never would come out right. By and by I learned though, and I write to 'em ever' year. You know, Joe, I reckon "thank you" is 'bout the two most powerful words a man can say, and I sure do wish I'd a said 'em a whole lot more when I had the chance. Those chances, they ain't a comin' back though. A whole lot of "thank you's" never got said, and that's that, but some things a man just got to live with.

Those christian wimmin, they remember me ever' Christmas, Joe. They know my name and they spen' a little time ever' year just a doin' somethin' nice for an old body that never did nothin' to deserve it. Even when there's no gif', they writes the purtiest words you ever did hear. That's how I come to know the Lor', Joe. They teaches me a little bit ever' year and I done learned a lot by now, but I sure do wish I knew a whole lot more. They say the Lor' is a makin' a place for me in the mighty kingdom. I can't say what kinda place the good Lor' would be makin' for a soul like me, but I reckon it'll be a lot like this one. I can't complain though, Lor' knows I don't deserve any better. I only hope it's a little closer to the sun. I reckon it will be, away up yonder.

There's one more gif' those ladies done sent me, Joe, and I want you to have it. It's a picture of the Savior, painted by hand on a genuine piece of ivory. I'm not sure I understand all of it, but the way I hear, it's just 'bout the most important gif' the good Lor' ever gave. I know it done me a whole

123

lot of good over the years, and I reckon it'll do some good for you too. You keep it nearby when the winter get real col' and it just might add a little sunshine to your soul.

I done wrong, and I can't deny it. Lor' knows I ain't a gonna do wrong no more, but I done wrong and I spent the last sixty one year feelin' sorry for it. I got triple life, Joe, and it seems like that just 'bout say it all. I lived one life before I came here, I done lived another one right here in this cell, and if the good Lor' see fit, I guess there's another one a waitin' for me.

I'm a gonna lay me down to rest now, Joe. I hope the good Lor' lay his hand on you, and I hope you learn to make the best of the life you have left. Seems the body is extra col' tonight, and I guess I done said all I need to say, except for one thing. Thank you, Joe, for your time.

SNOWSTORM by Maxine Fluegel

Our travels led to blowing snow,
Yet we had miles and miles to go.
We spied a snowplow up ahead.
"We'll make it now," my husband said.
But even though the road was clear,
We couldn't see afar or near.
We thought we'd try to stop awhile,
And then we saw the huge snow piles.
Again, we tried to drive on through,
And drove on for a mile or two.
Suddenly we saw buildings along the way!
What luck! We'd found a place to stay.

SUMMER IS A PAINTING by Maxine Fluegel

The house is quiet, the garden serene
Summer is sitting on a canvas of green
Painted with blossoms in colorful hues
Brilliant reds, yellows, oranges--soft blues.
A cardinal warbles his deep throaty song
While chickadees bustle and chatter along.
As bees are a-buzzing on flowers a-sway,
The kids down the street are laughing at play.
Summer is a painting where memories abound.
It is here that the brush strokes of life may be found.

MOM'S LYE SOAP by Kathy Kranz

In the fall of the year the summer kitchen used to be rather busy. We would butcher our own meat and render the pork fat in the old kitchen. When I was young I remember the times my Mom and I would make lye soap. My sisters were always in school when we'd make it and the job of wrapping the lye soap became my job. I remember Mom pouring it into her precious bread tins. When it would harden Mom would cut it and then my job came of wrapping it with brown paper and tying it together with white string. My hands would become red from handling the soap because it was harsh on my skin. Mom would then put it in the pantry and use it for washing clothes.

I thought that you might like the recipe so it goes as:

1 cup lye
4 cups cold water
3 cups rendered pork fat
1/2 cup ammonia
2 Tablespoons borax

Dissolve lye in the cold water being careful not to spill it as it becomes hot. Stir with a wooden spoon. Add borax now. Melt lard and cool and add to lye mixture about the same temperature. Add ammonia and stir 10 to 12 minutes or until it's thick like heavy syrup. Pour mixture into shallow pans. Let harden and cut into squares.

REAL PARENTS by Stan Miller

When I was but a sprite of a lad,
didn't matter who was my Mom or my Dad,
As long as I was fed and dry,
Happy and contented was I.

But a few short years down the road,
it started to matter who carried the load
'Cuz the words on each kids lips,
were my dad's stronger and more hip

And then another rite of passage,
with a twisted sort of rebellious message.
Old fogeys out of step and square,
Dad and Mom were really quite a pair!

Same message and love from days gone by,
wasn't understood by the teenaged guy.
And other parents he would get,
'Cuz the ones he had were all wet.

Still another change in my outlook,
as in marriage a wife I took.
And the lessons I'd been given to date,
were the ones we'd copied – me and my mate

We tried to copy the faith they had,
Yeah, I'm talking about my Mom and Dad,
who believe things work together for good
because it was God who said they would.

So now it matters who my parents were,
because they gave me a foundation sure.
And not every parent has the gift,
that is able the soul to lift.

So now that I've become a man,
I appreciate the Creator's plan,

127

of giving me when but a lad,
Godly parents like my Mom and Dad

But words are things, and a small drop of ink,

Falling, like dew, upon a thought, produces

That which makes thousands,

perhaps millions, think.

Lord Byron

SILENT NIGHT by Alice Ford

I am seventeen and the nation is at war. My mother's hair turned grey that year. She was forty five. The news from Europe was not good. Her son is a foot soldier on the front lines in Germany. He writes to us to send socks. His feet are moldy from the wet fox holes. It will soon be Christmas. We send sox, lots of sox's.   Nice warm ones. They are in wet snow and mud going from one line fence to another. From one hill to another.

He tells us "The Germans sit in the trees and shoot at us."

We send cookies in tin boxes and mother made a sponge cake and packed it in popcorn. He said "I got it in mint condition and the boys all had some. Just want you to know those chocolate cookies with the frosting were great"

He wasn't able to write much, but we were able to follow the newspapers. We knew who the commanding officers were. I remember my mother received a note from one of them along with a medal. It said, and I am not sure of the words, but it went like this.

"All the officers were killed taking hill #? And the men were told to be on their own and try and find base camp. Only three of them got back alive and your son was one of them."

Christmas has always been an important day for my mother. This is the only son she has, and this is the first Christmas he is not at home. The fact is she doesn't even know for sure where he is. She can't even be sure he is well. When his letters came they have words cut out and sometimes whole sentences are gone. He tells us what to watch for in the papers. Even to read his letters we first have to decipher the code he is using.

This is the story he told us after he came home all in one piece.

The day before Christmas the fighting had been so intense. Both sides in fox holes shooting at one another from very close range. Evening had fallen and the shooting continued. From somewhere they could hear music.

It was Silent Night. He said, " It became so quiet from both sides, not a shot was fired."

Our Lord's music is known throughout the world and that night it brought a small space of peace to the sons of great mothers. He said "When we looked around at the dark. The sky was filled with stars and the guns were silent.

LOVE IS By Alice Ford

Love is a human emotion
A very delicious devotion

That common sense defies.
With stars in the eyes

Goosebumps on the arm
You're in a state of charm.

Butterflies in the middle
Like the music of the fiddle

The body feels a stir within
The heart thumping like a violin.

The mind is a field of sand
The legs too weak to stand.

Rose colored glasses, wind in the hair
Do you look alright you suddenly care.

Is it real, or just no big deal?
How do you know? How do you feel?

No matter how hard you fell
Only time will be able to tell.

TRANSFER by Stan Miller

She'll change her name today.
Never more to carry mine.
She places her arm in mine this day.
Lord I continue to leave her in thine,
For she was only mine for a while.

The time has come to "give" her away.
Amidst tears of joy we can.
Believing in stewardship, I say,
Her Mother and I transfer to this man,
Our daughter, Gods precious gift.

KEY INGREDIENT by Stan Miller

The recipes of life are varied but the basic ingredients are essentially the same. There is one key ingredient.

Take several good friends, mix in a little laughter and a few tears. Add lots of love and season with other miscellaneous ingredients to taste. *Do not stop* here, because if you do life will be quite flat, although palatable. Stir in lots of prayer, Bible reading and singing praises to God, because the key ingredient to life *is* God.

Many people leave him out of the recipe and that is a mistake, like leaving out the key ingredient in any recipe, it spells disaster.

As I grow older and older
And totter endlessly,
I find I care more and more 'bout
Where I'll spend eternity!

Parody of a ditty in Dear Abby

CHILD OF THE LIVING GOD by Stan Miller

They say I'm just a fetus, a choice,
My soul knows better and it will rejoice.
For though my body is contorted, the pregnancy aborted,
I'm a child of the living God.

My Father says I'm not a choice, but love
Sent to earth from Heaven above.
To bring joy, whether a girl or boy
As a child of the living God

So although you don't want me here
Not my talents, abilities, laughter or cheer
This maternity sends me into eternity
I'm a child of the living God

Jesus said, "Bring the little ones to me,
Because of their faith they trust implicitly
I've prepared a place, thanks to mercy and grace
For the child of the Living God

"Whoever harms one of these little ones,"
According to the words of Gods only Son
Deserves to be thrown in the sea
For harming a child of the living God

So consider before you snuff out this little life,
The decision you make, o woman, o wife
These choices have voices
To praise their Father, the living God.

HARDKNOCKS by Alice Ford

My doorbell is ringing. I take children in during the day. It is six thirty and this is a mother at the door with her baby. I take the baby and tell the mother to have a good day. I am just taking off the snowsuit when the telephone rings.

Alice come over right away, Bill just shot himself Bill! Not Bill! He was just here in our back yard last night. He was laughing and kidding and he was just fine. The mind tumbles and whirls and the body is busy doing what has to be done.

I cannot leave the baby. It is late October and very cold. I put the snowsuit back on the baby.

We leave the house and I run with baby down the alley to my neighbor's house, all the time I pray to God that he is all the way dead. I know nothing about medical do's or don'ts.

His wife meets me at the door. She tells me he is ill the basement. She says, "I can't go down there, I am afraid, you go." I hand her the baby and tell her to call the doctor and our minister.

She tells me she already has. I turn and go down the steps to the basement. Bill is slumped in a in a chair way in the back of the basement sitting among the set of drum[s he bought for his son last Christmas.

I know that he is dead even though he looks just fine. I feel his pulse. Nothing. There is no blood. He has shot himself through the mouth and it came out behind his eye. He is just sitting there with his body leaning against a basement post. The doctor comes down the steps with his bag in his hands. He is easy and relaxed as he kneels down beside me taking Bill's hand to feel his pulse and says that he is gone. We stay for a moment taking it in. Bill's wife is waiting and we can hear the ambulance. The crew comes stomping down the steps talking loudly. I do not stay.

The minister is with Bill's wife and has skillfully taken charge. I take the baby, give my friend a hug and go home.

I seem to have words forming in my mind that have to be written down. I am still holding the baby in his snowsuit as I try to find a pen and paper. These words come as if through the air as I write them down.

I don't like October
With its flaming leaf and burning beauty
The eerie pale of winter threatens
The mind, the heart, and soul.
I shiver with every cold rain
And breathe deep the warmer days
In fear I'11 never have another
I don't like October
With Halloween and witches' treats
We make of it the best we can
Putting on a face of fun
The silly foolish kind of fun
We have when we're too tired.
October is so beautiful
With its red and yellow leaf
Like the breath of a young man
Snuffed out before its time
The useless death of human kind
Leaving wife and children behind
No. It's not for me. October flame.

The words come and I write them down. At that time I am not a poet or even a writer. I can rewrite them now, and give them rhyme, somehow I feel I should leave them alone.

In the aftermath as I listen to the town talk I hear what Bill was wearing. I hear reasons why he did it. I hear nasty talk about his wife. How she wasn't even home. None of it is true and I just keep my peace to myself. I knew them well, our children played together. We cannot always explain death. We just learn to live around it.

RAISING MIKE by Alice Ford

I am coming out of a sound sleep. Strange sounds are coming from the bathroom. It sounds like muffled cries from a baby. Yes, we have a baby. He is five months old and he is asleep in the buggy. Far too young to be in the bathroom at this time of day. Since he cannot walk or even crawl yet, how did he get out of the buggy? I ran to look in the buggy. He is not there. I ran to the bathroom, he is caught behind the toilet he cannot raise his heady and he cannot go forward. I have my doubts if his mom cuddled him, and called him precious. She more than likely said, "How did you get in here?"

Mike continues to grow his own power and strength. He could move, open or climb any project he had in mind. He was very good at taking things apart. Many bicycles, clocks, and later, cars.

Somehow we raced through his first live years. During this time he burned down the barn, trying to see where a mouse had gone. Mother again thought he was upstairs asleep. He shot all the tulip blossoms off a friends flower bed with his little bow and arrow. The fish that sat on top of the refrigerator came up missing, one day it was a dozen eggs on the floor broken.

His kindergarten teacher was all in a huff when she showed me a picture he had drawn of a men with all his parts. She is sure he was being abused. I asked her what she had asked him to draw. She said she had asked the class to draw a man. I said, "That is just what he did."

By the time he was in the first grade his teacher informed me that Mike was late for school every morning. Hnmm. I send him out of the door soon enough and he only has to walk two blocks. Since we had new fresh snow that very night, I sent him off to school, and then later traced his tracks. He had gone around every tree and bush. He had checked out some rabbit tracks and visited with every dog in the neighborhood.

Mike loved the creek that flowed through his grandfather's farm. He spent most of his young life fishing. If he caught some nice trout he would sell them to his elder friends in the village. Sometimes it would be April, long before fishing season opened.

When he was ten, I see him headed for my neighbor's with his BB gun. Before I could stop him, my dear neighbor had her arm around him and was showing him all the beautiful birds and their nests.

My husband knew how I worried about the creek. One day when they both came home from fishing my husband said, "You don't have to worry about the creek anymore. I threw him in. and he just pawed his way to the top."

One evening after bed time, my husband and I could hear the neighbor kids out whistling to one another on the streets. We were glad that ours were home in bed. Maybe I better check. No Mike, he had learned how to jump out of the 2| story window.

School was not his priority. He spent most of one grade sitting in a desk in the Principal's office. Mike explained it to me like this. "Well mom, somebody put a can of water on top of the door and when the teacher came in. I am the one that laughed."

There is more to that story. The Principal called me to say that Mike had etched his name in his desk. "What are you going to do about it?" All I could think of was. "Do you want me to come and sit with him too?" When he was fifteen one of my dear friends came to me and said, "How is our Mike doing?" I knew then he was getting a lot of help. Yes, sometimes it takes a village.

I love being a writer. What I can't stand is the paperwork.

First drafts are for learning what your novel or story is about.   Bernard Malamud

PILOTO'S GRANDDAUGHTER by Jennifer Tahtinen

The smooth gray sky was once again saying goodbye to the fading soft yellow moon. On the far side of the pasture filtered streams from an eager sun reached through tall dark pine trees. I was happily pulling tufts of sweet green grass from the earth's plate, chewing until full flavor permeated my tender equine mouth. All my homes have been good, but this one is best. I possess complete contentment.

Suddenly the quiet peacefulness was interrupted; off toward the east woods my cupped ear caught a subtle rustling. A moment later it stopped. I resumed pulling grass. Then another stirring alerted me. I raised my head. What was there? Only a deer with its wobbling dotted baby, not long in the woods, would speak stillness. As light conquered darkness the other animals became silent and sent me their inaudible messages of serenity. I swished my long dark tail and sauntered joyfully toward a favorite spot filled with fine lush grass.

It was then that I heard it — truck doors slammed! My front legs stiffened. I saw two people walk slowly toward my pasture. Unmoving, I watched, listening and sniffing.

A deep gruff voice spoke, "that horse'll get us a right good stack of hunerts."

A softer voice replied, "yup, she's a beauty."

Then I heard rattling. These nice people had brought me oats with molasses! She put the bucket down. The smell reached my wide discerning nostrils. I stepped forward and stopped. How tasty! I swallowed appreciatively and again dipped my head into the pail.

A heavy thud pounded my neck. I jerked. Moving above me was a heavy rope; she was trying to get it around my neck! I felt a powerful hand grab my long full mane. A fist dug into my side. I heard the clunk of a heavy chain. I tried to move. I could not move!

"Git git'er," he shouted.

I kicked. I jerked; I snorted with my nostrils wide. Again I kicked. Only air moved as my hard feet made a desperate effort to escape. But he was at my head — not my back! His hold was mean. He hit me with the chain and pain sliced into me. Ugly words spilled from his mouth. Then she slapped me with that rope. The hurt traveled all down my side. I tried to twist away through their commands, "quit — steady — whoa." I angled my head left, then, right — my eyes widened and my nostrils flared. My heart was pounding. Near exhaustion, I caught a slight weariness also creeping into him. The rope slipped from my back! Angry, he grabbed my mane more tightly, holding me with two hands. I whimpered with hurt.

"Got'er — now I got'er," he breathlessly hissed.

No more fight was to be found in me; I stood defeated.

With no warning, deep from somewhere within, my grandfather, Piloto's image appeared. I heard those words he spoke to me while I was yet a filly in the canyons of Peru. His words of long ago sounded in my head. I remembered. I remembered all that happened back then. His voice became loud,

"Fight when you must and never, never lose!"

With his image before me, I pulled. I pulled with all the fierce fighting strength of the well-muscled stallion who was my grandfather. Frantic and finding myself near exhaustion, I could hear his words but could move but a small step. Again, his voice boomed
"Pull, my precious! Your shoulders, your wide strong chest, my precious! Your Peruvian Paso strength is there — in the shoulders."

"Pull! Pull! Pull harder!" he demanded. As rivulets of piercing pain coursed through me his ethereal image vanished. I felt clumps of mane ripping from my neck and moved forward despite the anguish of tear after tear and more tearing leaving only short frizzled crimps.

Breaking free, I ran in saboreando -full open! My narrow chance of freedom had worked! The soothing morning air gently consoled me as I reached the far pasture. Heavy labored breaths slowly diminished and, once more, I was safe. I stood tall with regained dignity. I turned to watch the two walk toward that truck. He spit on my ground. Hanging from his hands were gobs of long strands of my dark beautiful mane. Truck doors banged shut. A sputtering motor caught and I saw the truck pulling its long rusty cattle trailer disappear down the road.

I bent my head once again seeking nourishment from the green grass. The sun had brightened as a new day made itself known. From near the stable I heard a familiar whistle signaling feed time! Even from this distance I felt her volumes of love. Showing myself beautiful—despite the ruined mane, I hurried in my paso llano gait toward her. Moving toward the stable my thoughts returned to the terror of earlier. I now realize that my grandfather-the great, legendary Piloto had taught me well; and, for that, I am so very grateful.

The act of creating a poem is like falling in love with life.

It takes 10 years to become an overnight success. Alice Yehudi

Far and away the best prize that life has to offer is the chance to work hard at work worth doing. T. Roosevelt

You can't get much writing done by starting tomorrow

THE PINK KITCHEN   by Alice Ford

I am now grown and yes even old. I realize that my mother must have been a very strong lady.

She did not look like a strong person, just a little slip of a girl, with pretty black wavy hair, maybe one hundred fifteen pounds.

My father was in the Hardware business with his father before the great depression. They sold John Deer machinery and Ford cars. By the time the depression was well into the sixth year, not much was selling. To keep afloat, my father had mortgaged the very nice house they owned in town.

The year was 1935. The nice house we lived in had running water, an indoor bathroom, handsome over-stuffed leather chairs, and a large dining room. My brother and I could walk to school.

I can imagine the terrible shock when he had to tell her they had lost the house and would have to move to his father's farm into a house that had not been lived in for years.

I was seven, and had no idea what all the fuss was about. I only knew we moved to this wonderful place with trees in the yard, a room of my own and cows.

I was too young to have to carry water and I rather enjoyed the outhouse. Seven-year-olds have no thought about winter, this little building known as the outhouse had Hollyhocks all around it and a gentle breeze from the flowers made it all smell good to sit there and contemplate someone else washing the dishes.

I do remember some things that probably upset my mother. When it rained, the rain came in under the north door, right through the house and out the back door. I remember having blankets over the windows and door to keep out the cold.

We always washed clothes on Monday. In the winter the clothes hung all around the house. I cans still see the minister from the local church sitting by the stove with the towels just touching the top of his head. My mother never could understand why he always came to visit on Mondays.

My mother set about to make the house a home for her family. She needed paint. We didn't have any paint. My father found some cans of old paint in the store. It was called Muresco. I have no idea how Muresco was spelled. It was thick and pink. The pink was pretty and it covered well and we had the most beautiful pink kitchen.

I always loved our pink kitchen. It makes me think of fresh bread baking, chocolate cake with thick butternut frosting and a tall glass of milk. Boy, that was really living for a seven year old.

THE SUN IS SETTING by Alice Ford

I am glad to be among the old
So many memories to be told
Past emotions to unfold
Feeling the joys I could not hold
The childhood games and schemes
Now tucked away as only dreams
The ice shed and the sawdust pile
On hot days it was a perfect place to play awhile

On the clothesline the weekly wash hung
While she worked my mother sung
Songs she learned when she was young
From the windows freshly washed curtains hung
Once a year we cleaned the rugs
Rid the house of smells and bugs
Then all of a sudden we were all grown
The time had come to be out on our own

I remember the very first kiss
At seventeen a very young Miss.
He told me in the rain would   melt
Stirred emotions I had never felt.
I knew him long before that day

From fun we had along life's way
Skating to the waltzing tune
In the fun warm days of June.

It was forever, right from the start
We kept our vows close to the heart
Knowing that we would never part
We were young maybe not too smart.
Five children came along in time
Had to try and save a dime
Lots of things we had to learn
Pleasures in life we have to earn.

Our sun is setting now in the west
We have tested all, and learned what's best
Our memories are stored with gold
Smiling faces, it is love we hold.

DEAR MOTHER by Alice Ford

Dear Mother you gave me a path
When I left it you showed wrath
I never could learn to do math
But I learned not to sass.

You always gave respect, and expected it back.
This is the thing that kept me intact,
Sometimes even blistered my back
You taught me to cook, clean, and mend.
How to hold life, never to bend.
To give, to love, and to lend.
Such a great mother and friend

This I have learned about you.
You're one in a million or two.
God gave me the best he could find,
The greatest of your kind.

SAVING ROSIE by Tina Widell

The wind blew in the dark clouds. The weather man on the TV was reporting the coming storm. My mind was consumed with thoughts of my big sister Rosie. Rosie was smart, beautiful, kind-hearted, and about to get hurt. The storms in her life would resemble a destructive hurricane if she kept going on her current path. Rosie had a high profile job in a computer company. With it came the high profile paychecks. Like so many smart beautiful kind-hearted women, she didn't know she could be an unsuspecting target. I had a plan and our little sister Peggy was my accomplice.

At that moment my phone rang. "Hi, Rosie." I tried to sound cheery. "Dan and I are going out for a few more wedding things. Want to join us?" She sounded so happy. I thought for a minute.

"Sure. I'll be there in 10 minutes. Is Peggy coming, too?" We could not miss this opportunity.

I knocked on Rosie's door. "Oh, come in! Come in! I'm so excited!" Rosie beamed. Dan and Peggy were already there and sitting on the couch.

"Hi, guys," I said, trying to conceal my emotions, making eye contact with Peggy.

"Are we ready to go?" asked Dan.

We arrived at the mall and went straight to the big department store. Rosie was beaming. She looked at dresses to wear on their honeymoon. She would need formals and casuals on the cruise. Dan looked around over the racks. His eyes rested on something far away. I followed them. He excused himself saying he was going to men's wear.

"Rosie." I whispered. "Come with us."

"Why?" Rosie asked.

"Because if you really go through with this wedding, you will be sorry," Peggy whispered.

"But Dan is the one! I've waited 20 years for this! I've kept my virtue for this! You just don't want me to be happy! Just because your marriages didn't work...!"

"That is why we are saving you from this! Our marriages taught us something that you haven't learned yet and we are going to teach you before it's too late!" I snapped.

Peggy and I each grabbed one of Rosie's arms and hurried after Dan. There he was, on the other side of the store, with the woman that Peggy and I had seen him with before. She was dressed as stylishly as Rosie. We watched from behind a clearance rack as he kissed the woman, long and deep. Rosie's mouth dropped open. Tears filled her eyes and her cheeks turned a fiery red. "Who is that?" she whispered angrily, her eyes flashing through the tears.

"Dan's rich booty call is our guess," I said. "You both knew about this and didn't tell me?"
"Would you have listened?" Peggy asked.

Rosie sighed. "I guess not."

"Come on. It's time to call him out." The three of us held hands and emerged from behind the rack. We stood together behind the woman where Dan would see us. He did. A shocked look crossed his face and the woman turned to see us. "Rosie."

Dan stammered "Why aren't you looking at dresses?"

"Who are they, Dan?" asked the woman. Dan glanced at her and looked back at us without giving her an answer.

"So now you know," he said to us.

"Know what, Dan?" the woman asked. I let go of Rosie's hand and went to the woman. I put my arm around her and led her to where Rosie and Peggy were standing. As we walked I said, "My sister here is Dan's fiancée."

144

"What!" the woman shouted in anger. "I am Dan's fiancé!"

"A little short on cash, are you, Dan?" I asked cynically. "So, which one was supporting the beer and pot?" The fiancés shot me a shocked look and then stared back at Dan.

Dan stared at the four of us lined up in front of him, his two fiancés standing hand-in-hand throwing daggers with their eyes. Shoppers around us stared. It seemed they were waiting for an answer too. Dan looked around at all of them and then back at us. He simply turned on his heels and walked away. The crowd applauded.

Rosie sighed and broke into sobs. Peggy and I put our arms around her. The other woman then put her arms around us. We looked at her. She had mascara trails running down her cheeks. "Thank you," she said. "I had no idea." I nodded looking sympathetic. She walked away.

Peggy and I took Rosie home. She sat speechless the whole way. Back in her living room, she asked, "How did you know?"

"We saw him several times. I saw him when I was out with my friends in the bar. Smoking, drinking, bragging about his rich girls," Peggy said.

"I saw him with her in the coffee shops, sneaking drinks from a flask in his pocket," I added.

"I am blessed to have you two as sisters!"

As we all know, the inside of a writer's head resembles squirrels nests more than they do neatly arranged file cabinets. Margaret Atwood

FRUGAL by Alice FORD

Frugal rules the day
Why are we this way?

Life was not funny
Without any money

When the cupboard is bare
And there is nothing to wear.

Creditors knock at the door
Of pennies we give them three or four.

Frugal rules the day
That is why we are this way

Find a penny, pick it up
Broken dishes, save the cup.

Break a shoelace, make a knot.
Resole a shoe, mend a sock.

Frugal rules the day
That is why we are this way.

THE BENCH by Alice Ford

The local cemetery lay at the top of the hill behind our house. The road went around and winding up the hill but someone had built a stile over the fence that made it a short walk into the cemetery.

I have a sister in that cemetery. She drowned in the river. Every spring when the lilac tree was in full bloom my mother would cut a few of the lilacs and put them in a can and send me to the cemetery to place them on her grave.

This would go on every few days until the lilacs were gone.

In this cemetery someone had placed a cement bench, I had to be under seven years old, more than likely five and six. I remember being intrigued by this wonderful bench. What a wonderful idea to have a bench where we could sit or play for a while. Throughout the summer my friends and I would make the trip to the cemetery. We never really played there. It just had this aura of quietness.

I remember another part of it. Another neighbor had a few pigs in a pen we had to pass. That year the Swine flu was very bad all over the city, and since we children connected the Swine flu with the pigs, we always made it a big deal to walk a long way away from the pen.

This was brought back to my mind this past year when we again had The Swine flu bug.

When Charles and I were chair people at the park in Swan Lake, we had the club buy three benches to set around the park as we had so many people that walked the park and the benches gave them a chance to sit down and rest.

It was funny sometimes as the benches would get moved to different locations. We finally had to bolt them down to the cement.

There is something about a bench that just invites us to sit down for a while and enjoy the world around us. Maxine Fluegel caught that for the front of our book, "Come Read With Us," and I have always admired it. The huge trees in the background and the green grass give us peace.

NOISES IN THE NIGHT by Alice Ford

What is worse than the drip, drip, drip of the faucet in the night? You may be in a different room, doesn't matter, you still hear the drip, drip, drip that keeps you awake. You're going to fix it in the morning, when morning comes you get up and the day is busy and when you crawl back into bed and what do you hear? The drip, drip, drip of the faucet. One of these days you will fix that faucet.

Now it is winter and it is well below zero. Whatever is that noise? It sounds like the house is cracking. It is! How about that fan on the furnace. Does it keep you awake or are you use to it? The really jarring thing at our house is when the heat enters the ductwork it bangs into the side of the aluminum and sounds like it is tearing it apart.

I have a son in law that turns off all the clocks when he comes to our house for the night. We do have a clock that dings every hour, but I never hear it. We also have a bird clock and a Christmas clock. The microwave talks, the coffee pot talks the washer and dryer talk to me. The nice part of getting old, you don't hear them any more.

When we were at the lake in the spring the tree frogs held a conference every night and all day. Talk about the quiet of the woods? No quiet there. Sometimes it would get so bad that you just wanted to go out and kill everyone of them. I really did go out and check on them. They are so tiny and there is an army of them. It is better to just put a pillow over your ears and try and sleep.

One summer we had the most annoying noise coming from close by in the woods. I questioned the neighbors that had lived there longer than us. "Oh Yes, that is the Green Heron."

I had never heard of a Green Heron, now I am on the hunt and watching. One day coming into dock with the boat I happened to look up and there it was. On a limb. I couldn't believe they called it a Heron. He was as ugly and ugly as he could get. Short legged and it had the yellowest legs. Nothing like what I had imagined. This creature had a terrible sharp barking. Kyow. You don't know if it's a dog or a kid. I even thought it was a bobcat the first time I heard it.

There is another noise in the night that we have heard. The coyote. Just the howl of a single coyote isn't all bad, it may even be exciting, but when the howl is on the east of you, and another to the north, with another in the west, your hair begins to stand on end and it is time to leave.

Even worse than the drip, drip, drip of the faucet is a single mosquito buzzing near your ear in the dark of the night. You are awake right now. No one sleeps until it has been killed.

Yes, we did fix that dripping faucet. All we had to do was turn it in the right position. Now there is no excuse for not sleeping at night especially since we don't have any city traffic noise or police sirens.

If all else fails, try some hot cocoa.

THE VIOLET by Jennifer Tahtinen

(For my Youngest Sister)

A delicate little purple flower
Sings far back in the awakening woods.
Almost unseen-nestled next to a decaying log-
Its song faint, but heard, by those
who see the loveliness
and realize this violet has a name:
It is Paula.

WINTER DANCE by Jennifer Tahtinen

They began their lovely, delicate dance
   dressed in frilly white.
Others jubilantly joined
twirling to the rhythm of silent music
Urging countless more to attend
   They continued this winter celebration.
White garbed swirling dancers
   Dominated the air.
As time passed they became a frenzied blur.
Until, finally, all were spent with exhaustion
and, in white heaps, upon the quiet ground,
   they slumbered
while the weary sky resumed its calm.

FROST by Jennifer Tahtinen

Tall ships listing in peril
Waves billowed high
Overhead a dark, unrelenting sky
A shore in the distance
But not a person in sight
Nature's art on my window
This cold winter night.

JESUS' KNEE by Tina Widell

I laid my head on Jesus' knee

In hopes that He would come to me.

Not one word did I speak

For He knows my faith is weak.

The scars bleeding on my heart,

The scars from every dart,

He could wholly heal

As before Him I kneel.

Evaporate all the unshed tears,

Comfort unrelenting fears,

Fill the empty space with love everlasting.

Fill my heart with the love of a king.

The most valuable of all talents is that of never using two words when one will do.
Thomas Jefferson

Life is like a bicycle. To keep your balance you must keep moving.

Albert Einstein

LIFE BEFORE TELEVISON by Alice Ford

I'm going to tell you a little bit about life in 1936. You recall a depression that took hold in 1928 and 29. It didn't really reach our house in Wisconsin until about 1935.

Even then we must have been rich among the poor because my brother had a bike and I had a pony. My brother was four years older than I and he enjoyed having his own kind of fun. When he taught me how to ride his bike, we started at the top of a hill, he gave it a push and I was riding in seconds, screaming all the way.

He taught me how to ride a horse the same way. He tossed me to the top of our big work horse and slapped the horse with a whip. The surprised horse galloped across the field at break neck speed with me screaming and hanging onto the mane.

My little pony was easy after that. We didn't know what a saddle was. We just rode bareback and barefoot. Yes, barefoot we didn't have shoes either. I did have a pair of shoes that were a bit small and had the cover of a Montgomery Ward's catalog for enforcing the sole. The shoes were saved for church or school.

Now the haymow was the place to play. My brother had tied a rope up to the ceiling of the barn and we could climb to a ledge along the side, grab the rope and swing out over the hay and drop.

The summer heat brought a reason to make root beer. The big copper boiler was brought in and the mixing of the root beer and the bottle capper. Then the finished root beer needed time to work. It was laid in rows under a bed in the upstairs where it was very hot. At haying time it was brought out and lowered into the well pit to cool.

We lived on a farm just a quarter of a mile from a school house. Because our farm was in a different county we had to walk the three mites to the school in our county. My brother would take his bike, but I walked it cross country. Crossed the creek, the railroad tracks and a small wooded area to a friend's house.

152

We often had tramps from the train come to outhouse asking for food or work. My mother never turned them away. She would set them a pan of water and soap out on the lawn, and take them a plate of dinner.

Because so many people were out of work, the table was always filled with people. My grandfather lived with us. We had a hired man that worked for his board and room and $9.00 a month. We also had a hired girl that worked for board and room for $3.00 a month.

If you were seven or ten, the farm is a wonderful place. I wanted to milk cows like my brother. Dad let me have this old cow named Annie that only could be milked from the left side. Annie and I became good friends and I continued to milk her night and morning until the day came that we could no longer keep her.

My grandfather had his own area where he had a sawmill. This meant a pile of boards and logs. It became my special play place. I would pretend it was a ship and I was the captain. I would travel the world by sea. He also had an old Studebaker car that sat among the tall grass, and I would get in a drive that from the Pacific coast to New York City. I would even take my baby sister with me in that old car and she would laugh and jump as I told her about all the things that we were seeing on our make believe trip.

Another great place to play was the ice house. During the winter the men would cut huge blocks of ice from the creek, and pile it in sawdust from the saw mill. When summer came it was the coolest place to play. It did have a drawback.

I can remember seeing big white rats that lived among them. I don't think I have seen a white rat since. Makes me wonder if we still have white rats? I nearly forgot to tell you that we made our own paper dolls from the Montgomery Ward catalog. I would cut out the person, then fmd a dress to cut out to fit her. We even made boy dolls.

Even at the age of eight we still had lots of work to do. We had this big berry patch right beside the house. It was my job to do the picking of these nice big raspberries. You know that sometimes they had an ugly stink bug in them. I wouldn't eat them until I was a lot older.

My brother and I would gather butternuts in the fall and pile them on the roof of the chicken house. Before Christmas my mother would get out the hammer and open them and my brother and I would pick out the meat. If we could get it out whole that was a plus. It was my job to sell pints of nutmeats to the rich people and we would get a much as $10.00 for a whole quart and $5.00 for a pint.

On washday mom would put the big copper boiler on the big old kitchen wood stove and she would boil the white clothes to get them clean. Even the soap was made out in the back yard. The clothes dried on the lines outside, and in the winter she would put up lines in the house. Then came the ironing. We had to iron evenings. My mother started me on the handkerchiefs first.

Outside beside the garden stood the two-hole outhouse. One hole was made smaller for the children. For paper we had last year's catalog or the papers from a box of peaches. You had to wrinkle that catalog paper to get it soft enough.

I rather enjoyed the outhouse. On a nice sunny warm summer day you have no thought of what winter is like. Our outhouse had Hollyhocks growing all around it and with a gentle breeze blowing. It all smelled good to sit there and contemplate someone else washing the dishes.

FATHER AND THE HORSE by Alice Ford

Handing her father a nickel, Kathy said, "Daddy buy me a horse." Nickels were hard to come by for dad right then, so the horse had to be promised for another time, after she saved a lot more nickels.

This four-year-old could not be put off forever. She saved those nickels, and enlisted her older brother to help save.

He was a better saver than she was at that time, and she knew it. They even convinced the baby brother to put all money in the small bank for the horse.

Kathy was seven when dad and the three children found the horse they wanted to buy. The children counted out all the dollars and cents and they had one hundred dollars.

The auction was a real nerve racking affair. There were other children at the auction that wanted the same horse. Maybe they had more money.

The auctioneer was up to ninety, ninety-five. Dad says ninety- nine. The auctioneer is still calling for more. Right here the children knew they had lost the horse and headed into a nearby woods to cry.

Dad was stronger, he stood his ground and the horse was his.

Now we had some happy children and a horse. The horse opened up a whole new world for us. We needed a little land, a little barn, fence posts, and wire. This horse needed hay and oats. It wasn't long before we had a small farm going.

Kathy would stand on the fence board and put the halter on the horse. From there she could jump on and ride. They rode bareback as it was a long time before this family could afford a saddle.

It's a good thing that she had an older brother. A horse comes with two ends. A front that needs food and a back end.

That horse was better than a babysitter. It kept the children and the neighborhood kids busy for hours. They could jump on it or off of it from any direction. The horse didn't seem to care.

When the children were old enough they joined a saddle club. They would ride the horse to and from the practice field.

One afternoon a drunk saw the horse and headed right for it. They were off the road. I suppose he was looking at them and didn't realize where he was heading.

Mom and dad were both at home when the telephone rang. Someone was saying the children had been hit by a car just past the bridge. Dad left the telephone dangling and was out the door and into the car. In the hurry and fear of what he would find, he backed over the new tricycle that the three year old had left in the driveway.

I think God gives fathers some superior force to help them at a time like this. He got out of the car, untangled the remains of the tricycle and hurried on. He could hear crying as he drove up. That was a good sign.

The horse was on the ground. Things were not to be easy. Both front legs of the horse had been broken. The policeman let father get the children in the car and off to the doctor before he put the horse out of its misery.

The people-friendly horse named Patsy could never really be replaced. The children both healed and the tricycle wasn't a total loss either. The same strong hands that drove those heartbroken children home, applied force in just the right places and soon the tricycle was running again. The tricycle made it through another baby although it always had a cockeyed look about it.

A writer once got so discouraged by the failure of one of his novels that he gave up writing completely, and became an agent in the New York Customs House. Many years after his death his books and stories gained great critical acclaim and recognition. Perhaps you've heard of this man. His name was Herman Melville, and the book that was received so poorly was Moby Dick (News clipping - source unknown)

BREAD MAKING by Kathy Krantz

During the course of my mom's life she made many a loaf of bread and many a pan of buns. When my mom, Violet was 8 years old she had learned how to make bread using a wood stove. It had a top shelf, the warming oven, where mom put the bread to raise.

Bread had to be made year round so even in the hottest days of summer the cook stove had to fired up. In Mom's family there were eight children and Grandma. I don't know how many loaves she made at once when she was growing up but it had to be quite a bunch.

Before Mom went to the nursing home she gave me her oldest cookbook. One day while searching in her cookbook I found her recipe for buns. I wished that Mom could be here to make the buns again. In the choruses of my mind I could picture Mom standing by me and saying. "Kathy you can do it. What have you got to lose by trying?" With that I rolled up my sleeves and proceeded to try to make the bread. Wa La! I did it!

I am not as good as Mom was at it but she started way younger age than I did.

This had not been my first attempt at trying to make bread. When I was married to my first husband I bought some frozen bread dough. I didn't have a bread tin so I used a 9X9 cake pan. I put it in the oven to bake and was tired so I fell asleep. The next thing I know is that my husband was asking what I had in the oven'? I took it out and after it had cooled he dropped it from arm's length down onto the floor. It didn't even dent and we had lived in the basement of a house and the floor was cement. We could have used that loaf of bread for a cornerstone for a house!

Ah, the joys of making bread. I like the feel of the dough in my hands. My great great grandpa came over from Norway. When he lived in Norway he was a baker there. They didn't have electricity and he had to stir 100 pounds of flour plus all the other ingredients by hand. Yes, Mom came by it naturally.

FISHY PROPOSAL by Pat Solomonson

They were guests of friends at an elegant country club party. Champagne, soft lighting and romantic music. Danceable music. When they weren't gazing across the table into each other's eyes they were gliding, ever so effortlessly, around the dance floor.

It was New Year's Eve and their courtship was about to enter its fourth year. The relationship had overcome many obstacles.

She was a widow with five children. He had long been a carefree bachelor.

It wasn't supposed to work. "Bachelors are too set in their ways," she had been warned by well-meaning friends.

She was a city girl. His roots were in rural Wisconsin. He was the youngest of ten. She was the eldest of two.

Ignoring all the obstacles, they managed to "seize the moment" in their very different and very busy lives. They made time for real dates, for dining and dancing. Oh, how they loved to dance!

He taught her how to ski and they soon discovered that swooping down a mountain together had a joyous rhythm all its own.

Summer weekends at her lake cabin brought out the handyman in him. First major project, a screen house in need of finishing. It became his bachelor pad. (Or "man cave" as they say now.)

Her children found him to be a ready source of information and ingenuity. He was infinitely patient, considerate, and respectful of them.

On those warm summer evenings, sitting quietly by the shore of the lake, they would gaze at the stars and listen to the loons. He knew a lot about nature and the galaxies. They discovered they shared a deep faith in God.

He liked to fish. To her, fishing was boring. When he invited her to go along she usually declined.

Befitting his bachelor lifestyle, he required periods of solitude. He enjoyed being out on the lake alone. Fishing was an opportunity for him to commune with nature. And to ready himself for the next onslaught of boisterous, scrappy kids.

An incurable romantic, he often left little notes, silly little handcrafted rhymes for her to find on the fridge after he'd left to run an errand in town...or to go fishing.

As the New Year's Eve revelers all around were readying for a raucous welcome to 1972, he took her hand and smiled lovingly through the flickering candlelight, a smile that always touched the very depths of her soul

Would he finally do it? Would he pop the question?

His gentle smile now becoming more of a silly grin, he looked her straight in the eye, then said, "I think this should be the year we either fish or cut bait."

UPDATE: We decided to fish.
It's now been 40 years since we acquired that lifetime license.

I've learned that there is no elevator to success. You have to take the stairs.

Conversation means being able to disagree and still continue the discussion. Dwight MacDonald

---

CAMERA CLUB STORIES by Walt Fluegel

Alex of the camera club told me stories about two different doctors. The first story was about his own physician.

After Alex got his annual physical exam, the doctor went over the results. Shortly after that, the doctor announced he would no longer be in town and was leaving to go elsewhere. Alex had been his patient for many years, and in his anxiety about finding a new doctor, Alex asked, "What is going to happen to me now?" With a straight face but a twinkle in his eye, the doctor replied "Oh, you will eventually die." Fortunately, Alex knew his doctor had a sense of humor, and after the initial awareness of the joke they parted company with a laugh.

Alex met a retired ophthalmologist while on a hike. They got to talking and when the conversation drifted to the doctor's occupation, Alex related that he had floaters in his eyes from time to time. He also told the doctor he noticed a curious thing. Whenever he used a netting to keep the bugs away from his face the floaters seemed to disappear. It was another one of those moments when Alex noticed the expression on the doctor's face. The doctor said, "Boy, I wish I would have known about this years ago, I would have made a fortune selling netting to all those patients who had floaters. Twenty five bucks for the netting and consulting fees would have been great!"

The following has nothing to do with Alex it's just on the page.
There was a class reunion with drinks and goodies spread on the table and people milling around. Mike had not seen Bill for several reunions so Mike started the conversation.
Mike: Bill, have you tried this cheese concoction?
Bill: I tried it once and didn't like it.
Mike: Say Bill, they got some good wine over there.
Bill: I tried it once and didn't like it.
Mike: Tell me Bill, do you watch any sports -- baseball perhaps?
Bill: I tried watching a game once, boring, didn't like it.

The conversation was getting a bit frustrating with the same answer to other questions so Mike asked one more. Tell me Bill, how is your only child?

PLANE CRASHES NORTH OF LUCK WISCONSIN by Bob MacKean

Wreckage still missing after six years.

On May 1, 2003 a small plane was observed flying erratically just above the treetops near 280th Street west of Hwy 35. When the aircraft suddenly dove out of sight and didn't reappear, the observer rushed to the possible crash site. Searching in ever-widening circles, he was unable to locate any sign of the airplane or any piece of wreckage. Completely puzzled, he returned home to report the incident.

He met his wife at the front door. She had been wondering where he had been for so long. He sheepishly admitted that he had lost his birthday present. An expression of curiosity and disbelief spread across her face. She had been so diligent in selecting just the right gift. The salesman at the hobby store told her the Firebird XP radio-controlled model was their best-selling unit because of its performance and simple control system.

Earlier that day, he had opened his gift and thanked her profusely. The model was quickly assembled, a charge was pumped into the battery and a thorough pre-flight was performed to make sure everything worked. His wife asked if it might be too windy to fly but he assured her that it would just be a quick spin around the yard. The powerful electric engine literally pulled the plane out of his hand and into the air. It climbed slowly and responded to his every command. After an effortless circle, he turned it back towards himself for a landing but decided one more short flight wouldn't hurt. As the plane climbed out again it got caught up in the strong winds above the trees acting like a kite and blew ever-farther away. Every attempt to turn it back failed. In desperation he intentionally tried to crash it where he could pick up the pieces and reassemble it--but it was out of range and out of control. All he could do was watch it become smaller and smaller as it twisted and turned before disappearing from sight.

For nine long years now family, neighbors and friends have helped to find the beautiful, red Firebird but by now, it has probably decayed into the forest floor. There is a well-worn path to the probable area. There's always hope.

He has purchased another Firebird and says that there is no way you will ever see this one fly on a windy day.

CANADIAN ORDEAL By Bob MacKean

Four good friends graduated from high school anxious to get away from it all for a while. They had spent the winter building a camping trailer that would be their base camp for a fishing trip deep into Canada. With the trailer packed and two canoes lashed on top, it dwarfed the little Jeep pulling it. Parents came to say goodbye, each bringing treats for the boys to enjoy during the long trip to Lake Pokashcan, north of Kenora, Manitoba. With spirits high, they arrived at the lake just as planned but the plan was about to unravel.

The first day of paddling was into a stiff wind and the lake seemed a lot longer than it appeared on the map. With the one-foot waves, fishing was impossible so the evening meal they had anticipated all day would have to come from the trail packs brought along to supplement the many meals of fish we had planned. As the cook, I learned that "serves four" printed on a food pack actually means " barely two" when feeding four hungry canoeists and that a poorly built tripod, when bumped, could dump the whole evening meal into the fire. That first meal disaster caused my popularity to take a huge nosedive. With four "meals" gone the first day and our inability to catch any fish, the next two days we talked about turning back instead of completing the circle route as planned. It got so bad at one point that the ones that didn't take sugar in their coffee thought they should get sugar cubes to eat as a snack. It was getting pretty testy.

Somewhere near the "point of no return" we were staggering along a difficult portage when we were shocked to meet a party of two taking the same trip in the opposite direction. They had trusted an outfitter to supply their food. Bless them. They were snacking on what looked like a five-pound sack of raisins and asked if we would care for some. We traded trail information and as we parted, I'm sure they were surprised when we handed them a near-empty bag. We had all stuffed our pockets. Our luck had turned.

162

That evening we caught fish for supper and also discovered a use for all the flour brought along for batter. When mixed with smashed sugar cubes and water it could be shaped into thick pancake-looking biscuits After browning them in a dry frying pan they got so tough you could carry them in your pocket without breaking them. For the rest of the trip if we got hungry, I mean really hungry, you could pull one out and chew on it. We affectionately called them "hard things". At our high school reunion, fifty years later, we all had vivid memories of this trip, especially those biscuits, and had a great laugh.

Q. What can a young investigative reporter learn from a turtle and a woodpecker?

A. A turtle makes progress only when he sticks his neck out, and a

woodpecker chips away until he finds his morsel. W Fluegel

You can't get writer's cramp if you have writers block.

There is no money in poetry, but then there's no poetry in money either. Robert Graves

The best writing is rewriting. E B White

GRANDMA GETS BUSTED by Pat Solomonson

My air travel days may be over but there's excitement, or maybe it's just the thrill of the risk in those memories. Thanks to daughter Mary, who works for a major airline, I enjoyed the privilege of flying cheaply for many years.

With my titanium knees, the four large stainless steel screws that are supposedly holding my spine together and now a brand new pair of nickel chrome shoulders, I simply expect to set off major alarms. Then I would be escorted to the dreaded pat down area.

What those security people never realized is that my daughter had already thoroughly searched and confronted me regarding any questionable items in my luggage. All due to a few unfortunate incidents in the past.

It started when they confiscated a knife in my purse. I always carry a little paring knife for cutting up an apple or whatever. It was no great loss, because I did have a spare. I guess it was my decision to hide a spare knife in a different part of my luggage that first set off my daughter's internal alarm when traveling with me.

On one of our many trips to North Carolina to visit the granddaughters, I had packed all the fixin's for their favorite "monkey bread," including several cans of those pressurized biscuits. It seems every time I attempt to open one of those cans in my own kitchen I have to stand back and brace myself. It's either going to be a very large pop or something resembling a minor explosion.

Nevertheless, I did not anticipate what could happen when those cans were subjected to the difference in air pressure down there in the belly of the big bird. Yes indeed, those babies did explode, but muffled by all of the surrounding luggage, it was probably no more than a series of indistinct pops. No apparent witnesses, so I guess I lucked out.

As my husband, a private pilot, said after he had taken me up for my first ride in his little airplane (this during our courting days), "Well, we walked away from another one."

On another of those big bird airline trips with Mary, an alert regarding something suspicious in my luggage probably piqued the curiosity of other waiting passengers as my daughter's name was called on the PA system. She was ordered to report to Security there in the Raleigh-Durham airport for questioning about an item in our luggage.

Holding up an unmarked little glass jar containing what those security sleuths believed to be little brown seeds, they asked her to explain. She could not. So there in her presence they carefully opened the unlabeled jar and gave it the sniff test. Their determination? It was actually chocolate, not the illicit substance they had suspected.

Unfortunately, she told the questioners, she had not been aware of the little jar of chocolate sprinkles I had tucked into my suitcase. I had planned to use them for cookie baking with the granddaughters but we ran out of time. They tossed the jar and let her go.

To say that daughter Mary was exasperated with me is an understatement. Our travel plans would have been severely disrupted had I been cuffed, charged with drug possession and hauled off to the clink.

Too many people are ready to carry the stool when the piano needs to be moved.

I have learned to use the word impossible with the greatest caution. Wernher Von Braun

ADVENTURE OF YESTERYEAR by Kathy Kranz

Here's another saga about our old home! Yes, it's about the bird's eye view from a child's point of view. The home of my youth had dormer windows in the upstairs. They were big enough for me to crawl into and lie down and take a nap in when I was about 4 feet tall. I would go upstairs in the daytime and pretend that these dormer windows were a ship! I was the lady on the ship being taken captive by the pirates!

Oh yes, the eyes of a child. On my ship I became the lady of the hour all dressed in fine linen and silk. Adventure at high sea where the Captain asked me to escort him to a ball on shore at a seaport.

Dressed in fine linen? Nothing but the best for my lady, says the Captain. At the banquet where oranges, apples, pineapples and all sorts of good food which comes from exotic lands. Nothing but the best would do! My Captain was handsome in his blue coat with gold roping and white leggings! A big hat with white feathers was his headdress. Oh yes, the best money could buy. We danced and laughed with other people that were at the ball.

KATHY, KATHY!! K-A-T-H-Y. Alas! All too soon my dream would be cut short never to know the ending. My mother waking me up and scolding me for having had wasted another day when she thought I should have been helping her to pull weeds!

Now, those dormer windows are gone and I'll never get to know the end of that beautiful ball.

JUST HIT THE BALL by Bob MacKean

The following event takes place between 9:17 a.m. and 9:18 a.m. My first round of golf in the spring and I'm standing on the tee of hole number one in front of a crowd.

I scan the horizon as if I'm deciding where to hit the ball when actually that's the last thing I want to do right now. The fresh-mown expanse of grass spread before me holds a dread that won't go away unless I swing at that innocent, white ball waiting patiently on the tee right in front of me. Right now I'd like to fake some sort of stomach disorder, which wouldn't be far from the truth, and run to the bathroom telling my friends I'd meet them at the second hole - but I won't. As I look at the ball I notice that it seems to be teed up too high. Then I remember I did that so I didn't tense up and miss it entirely. It looks like at least two other foursomes are waiting to tee off and are getting restless. I don't recognize any of them, must be from the cities, all dressed up so nice. Probably spent the winter golfing down south somewhere. I should take a practice swing but it never helped before. Maybe a prayer would help.

God, If you would just guide this ball fairly straight down the fairway, not really far, even a hundred yards would be appreciated. Amen. I remember that God helps those who help themselves so I'm going to have to swing. I'll take a deep breath, let it out slowly, then let it rip. I just know I'm going to top it and it'll skitter through the grass stopping short of the women's tee but I guess it wouldn't be the end of the world if that happens. Sounds like I just set myself up for failure. I'm usually more positive. I might actually hit it good. There, I feel better. O.K. Deep breath. Line it up, keep the head down, elbows in and nice graceful swing. Ping! Oooow, that sounded good. I hope someone watched the ball.

I forgot to look up.

GROWING OLD CAREFULLY by Bob MacKean

While waiting outside a quilt shop we had spotted while driving along the north shore of Lake Superior I became aware of the rhythmic roar of the waves pounding against the jagged shoreline. The urge to explore

167

overcame me. The cool breeze gave me an unexpected chill so I grabbed my jacket and camera from the car before walking to the water's edge. I found an opening in the brush that revealed a steep path. I stopped in my tracks. In my younger days I wouldn't have given it a second thought, just gleefully scrambled down. But now many fears were holding me hostage. I saw myself lying at the base of the hill injured. How seriously would I be hurt? How long would it take to recover? Would I be permanently disabled?

Forcing these thoughts into a dark corner of my mind, I cautiously made my way down. The noise and beauty took my breath away. Four-foot waves crashed angrily against the ancient shore sending up a spray that almost reached me. To my left was an outcropping of huge boulders where two seagulls were enjoying the bright sun. Another wave of self-preservation swept over me as I moved from rock to rock over deep crevasses to get closer for a picture. As the larger waves crashed over the rock the gulls stood on, they seemed to know just when to spread their wings into the wind, then lift effortlessly until it had passed then glide gently back to their perch. How I envied such fearlessness and freedom.

After scanning the horizon for ships and taking many pictures I warily made my way back to the path remembering how I used to make a game of running along these rocks, trusting my feet to find a place to land. Was I brave then or foolish? I say brave. Now I'm older and cautious. Climbing up the hill seems so much easier and as I get to the car, she is coming out of the shop. She worriedly asks "Did I take too long? Did you get to see the lake?" I tell her how spectacular it was and ask her to come and look at it with me. At the edge she takes in sudden breath and asks "Were you down there?" I feel a wave of pride as I answer "You bet!"

FRAMING: A PERSONAL STORY (ABOUT A DEATH PANEL) by Walt Fluegel

An editor of a small newspaper was discussing a possible story concerning the school roof leakage. If not repaired it would take a big bite from the budget if there was too much delay. He said it was a matter of framing the issue. Should he slant the story about lack of funds, the architectural report, preventable maintenance in the first place, or a recent storm? It was potentially an important story but . . . I leave the rest for your imagination.

The concept of framing is always here because there generally is a difference of opinion depending upon a point of view. Little did I know that there is academic study on the topic of framing. Not only that, but for about 40 years now one major political party has made an intensive study of applying the most effective words, language or phrases to express their political philosophy. More about that later.

There are different parts of our society which are organized such as Catholics, Lutherans, Baptists, Jews, Republicans, Democrats, Lions, unions, fraternal organizations, and others. They are who they are because of some distant history, some founder, some set of rules or traditions and people who have the same goals. These organizations frame themselves. Some organizations in our country are benign and do not oppose others who have similar goals for their members. For example, do the Lions openly use language in opposition to the Kiwanis? However, in this country and other parts of the world we know that union and management, political parties, religious and ethnic groups are constantly stuck in battle with words or arms with their framing differences.

Let's use a few words. You have heard the expression, -- one country's terrorist is another country's Freedom Fighters. How about death tax vs. inheritance tax. Those are framing concepts. How about the discussion during the Affordable Health Care Act bill debate about Death Panels vs. end of life care? Now we are talking about something close to home and personal. To the opponents of the bill, death panels would decide the fate of granny in her final days. The use of the term death panels sends a powerful negative impulse, that adds to other negative impulses to make the entire bill some horrendous law. According to framing by the death panel proponents, I was on a "death panel."

169

It started when our family physician used the term "palliative care" after he saw the scans of Maxine's brain taken at the local hospital. We knew the term palliative care meant that her brain tumor would be terminal. But if we wanted to, there was a slim chance of successful treatment with radiation. We took that option, but with time the slim chance became zero and not successful.

Fast forward to Fairview hospital, a teaching hospital of the University of Minnesota. There were three doctors interested in Maxine's case. One doctor received new brain scans taken the night before and that I witnessed in the x-ray room. I could see the monitor as the technician did his work of taking the photos. I saw where two tumors were located. When the scanning was finished I remember saying to the technician, "I know you are not allowed to discuss anything with me. But I saw what you saw." He just nodded and then said I could follow Maxine's gurney into the elevator.

Before that final scanning, our grown adult kids, Margo and Grey and I had contacted a hospice person and she explained various options. We knew and understood the doctor's reports. In the meantime Maxine was hooked up to a deep intravenous tube a few days before and somewhat conscious but not communicative. She sometimes responded to questions but answers did not always make sense. My kids and I knew all alternatives and came to one conclusion. Hospice by definition was care until nature took its course.

So later we met with the doctors at Maxine's bedside after the talk with the hospice person. The doctors again asked Max various questions. At this time no matter what question was asked she repeated her name after each question. All we could do was to look at the doctors and they looked at us. The three of us indicated to the doctors that the IV tube be removed and I told them we were prepared to make the hospice arrangements. (Several years ago Max and I prepared an Advanced Directive just in case we needed it for an occasion such as this.)

The above is a blurry summary of the events but if you, whoever you are, who opposed the Affordable Health Care Act are inclined to think we, Margo, Grey and I were a death panel, -- your framing concept is heartless and cruel.* We all felt we had good information. We knew the facts. We were not pressured by the doctors or, had any doubts what two aggressive brain tumors were doing.

Because this is an article about framing an issue it might be up to you to flesh out the whole concept. Google - political framing - George Layoff - moral politics - liberal and conservative framing - to get a start on understanding how words, language, psychology, philosophy, dogma, and intent of an idea can shape what humanity does to its people. It cannot be summarized in a few pages. Max would agree with me.

*((You deserve all the expletives ever conjured for the deceptions you have foisted upon the American people during our debate on the merits of an issue in the docket for almost a hundred years.))

Either write something worth reading or do something worth writing. Ben Franklin

When we feel an impulse to use a marvelously exotic word, let us lie down until the impulse goes away. James A Kilpatrick

MOTHERING THEN AND NOW by Pat Solomonson

Of all the Mother's Day cards I've ever received, the one that stands out in my memory was the work of my son, Mark at age 7. His second grade class assignment was to design a very personal Mother's Day message. His handmade card, carefully printed with red crayon on blue construction paper, read simply, "Mothers are the ones who are always right."

Now in his 40s, Mark has become very adept at tuning me out, albeit with a loving wink, every time I remind him about that.

It's hard to take ourselves too seriously after we've spent a good chunk of a lifetime in the mothering role. One of many incidents my family won't let me forget revolves around the "boot camp bran muffins".

It was that very emotional experience of sending a young son off to the military. We were gathered at the airport for our final goodbyes as Scott headed for Marine Corps boot camp. As I hugged him for the last time, I quietly tucked a package under his arm. It was a fresh supply, packed "to go," of his favorite bran muffins.

"I can just see him now," mused my husband after the departure, "face to face with his drill instructor, when he's questioned about what he's got in that package."

"Muffins, Sir, muffins from my mother," he would dutifully reply as my labor of love was confiscated.

Mother's Day always triggers a flood of memories for me. As a stay-at-home mom in the days when that was the norm, I thought I had the upper hand over those little rascals, most of the time. I believe God gives every mother the required amount of psychic power to stay on top of things.

Prophetic moms will always recognize reports of pain in a small belly as news that the teacher has scheduled a test that day. I recall the day I gave my fifth grader the benefit of the doubt. His teacher called to check. "Pain in the stomach?" she snorted. "If you ask me, I think it's a pain in his Social Studies." Because the malady had run epidemic proportions that particular day, the teacher, one up on these connivers, rescheduled the test for a different date.

Maternal clairvoyance is even easier with very young kids. Like when your first grader swaggers home with a confident smile that means he's earned the respect of his peers. He plops his books on the table, faces you squarely, then announces in true 'big shot" fashion, "I told the teacher that you would...."

You know before he's even finished the sentence that he has volunteered your service to either, (1) provide 32 popcorn balls for the Halloween party, (2) accompany the class on their field trip to a farm, or (3) provide summer vacation board and room for the white rat that now inhabits his classroom.

While everyone knows that mothers hear all, see all and know all, there are times when we are caught off guard. We had a two-year-old acrobat who kept us all on our toes with his atrocious dinner table antics, all performed from varying positions in or on his high chair.

At one meal he suddenly stood up and fired a radish across the table, making a direct hit into his father's glass. He acted so quickly that none of us was aware of what was happening until we saw the splash of milk. This, of course, prompted much gleeful howling from all of his siblings.

Ah, the memories. I wish God's blessing on all the mothers who are still in the throes of raising children with the hope that you will treasure these years and not wish them away. You have the most important job in the world, and you only get one shot at it.

Special tribute is due also to the many grandmothers who are now sacrificing much of their own personal time of life to provide the care needed, at least for a while, by grandchildren. I stand in awe.

LESSONS MY DAD TAUGHT ME by Kathy Kranz

Growing up I didn't see much of my dad. When I did he was always working. Yes, I saw him at the supper table. I saw him in the fields working his land. I saw him milking cows. My dad was there for me and yet I didn't know my dad until I was married and we both lived in Clayton, Wisconsin in 1972.

Then my dad became my friend. Then I knew my dad as someone who loved to dance, go bowling and attend church. Then I knew him as someone who grew and harvested an eight acre garden. My dad always worked hard in his life. That much I do remember. Dad always working, working, and working until the day he died in December 1977.

Dad also taught me about finances. I remember him reading Kiplinger's magazine about what was the best car to buy in that year or what refrigerator was good to buy. Kiplinger's magazine often faced me as I was doing my schoolwork around the kitchen table. Dad read at it night while I did my schoolwork. Mom made Dad's lunch for work the next morning.

He went to bed at 9 pm every night and got up at 3 am every morning. He worked at Stella Cheese in Clayton, Wisconsin. He also had a farm outside of Turtle Lake, Wisconsin on Hwy 63. Like I said, Dad worked hard

Over the years of my own life I've implemented the ethics of working hard. Unlike my dad I became sick with schizophrenia and my health doesn't allow me to work as hard as I did when I was younger. However, I didn't let schizophrenia stop me from working as much as I am capable of doing. Mom always said that God helps those who help themselves. I've tried to work at the things this body will allow me to do. Another one of Mom's saying was where there's a will there's a way find the way.

Between Dad teaching me to work hard and mom being strong and teaching me to become independent and yes, some people call me stubborn. I have come to a place in my life where I can truthfully say I've

174

done my best. I was a divorced single mom for a long time and taught my children what dad taught me. Work and work hard. Each of my children has said to me they are glad that I taught them how to work. All three of them have always held down some type of job. Sometimes they have held down as many as three jobs at the same time.

Tonight as I sit here typing this up did I know my dad? The answer comes in the reward of a job well done. The answer comes when I lay my head down at night on my pillow and quote my dad as he used to say that he earned his salt today. The answer comes when the anniversary of his death comes around and I recall seeing him on the tractor out in the field plowing it up. The answer comes to me on a hot summer's day when people are out bailing hay and the smell of the flesh cut hay assails into my memory.

Did I know my dad? Perhaps you did. His name was Joseph Donatell of Turtle Lake, Wisconsin and later on Clayton, Wisconsin. I hope some of you knew my dad for he was always kind and thoughtful of others. Perhaps about my life someone would remember me in the same way I remember my dad...with love and honor and respect.

Yes Dad, you did earn your salt.

Tonight I'm reading a book 'Summers with the Bears.' by Jack Becklund. While reading this book I'm sitting here thinking about some of the wild life experiences I have had over the course of my lifeline of living on dead end roads. My experiences started in 1 993 when my husband and I purchased 5 acres of land in Barronett Wisconsin. My family lived there until June 1, 1998. From there we moved to Frederic, Wisconsin on an eight acre parcel on a dead end road.

The experiences that taught me to be cautious are in good stead for everyone. While we lived in Barronett some of the episodes that happened were the following. We had a dog named Shelton when we lived there and we got him as a young pup. We hadn't moved in long when Shelton got loose and chased a bear cub into the woods behind our neighbor's house. I started to go after Shelton when I realized that where there is a cub or two there might be a mama bear. I turned tail and went back into our trailer

175

house. It wasn't long before Shelton came running back into the trailer house too. Henceforth welcome to the wild life

Another time in Barronett it was a very hard winter and the wolves were out and about I was busy making supper when I heard howling outside. At first I didn't see anything and so I went back to frying chicken. A little while later I heard more howling. This time I could see one wolf OK I'm inside my house I'm not too afraid and soon the rest of my family would be home for supper. More howling and now there were three wolves. Just then my daughter came home from school and we surmised that it was our supper that they wanted. I shut off all the burners and waited for my two sons and husband to come home for supper. When they came home the three wolves left as they figured there were too many of us to outdo them. We had a half-cooked meal that night for supper but not one of us complained about it.

My Wishes for You by Boyd Sutton

I wish you everything that is good and gracious, loving and kind.

Black velvet sky glittered with diamonds on a dark night.

Blue sky and lazily drifting clouds on a sunny day.

Silence, but for the sounds of wind and nature.

Peaceful dreams when you sleep, warm comfort when you awake.

Strength to take you through a difficult day.

Safety in the arms of the one you love.

Whoever undertakes to set himself up as judge in the field of truth and knowledge is shipwrecked by the laughter of the gods. Albert Einstein

Faith will never die as long as colored catalogues are printed.

WINTER DANCE by Jennifer Tahtinen

They began their lovely, delicate dance
        dressed in frilly white.
Others jubilantly joined
twirling to the rhythm of silent music
Urging countless more to attend
        They continued this winter celebration.
White garbed swirling dancers
        Dominated the air.
As time passed they became a frenzied blur.
Until, finally, all were spent with exhaustion
and, in white heaps, upon the quiet ground,

WINTER SOLSTICE by Denis Simonsen

Winter Solstice
No longer guided by the sun,
Heads bow low.
Genetic dreams are anchored
Beneath the frozen snow.

Assignment: How would you like to be invisible for one hour in a place of your desire?

ON BEING INVISIBLE: TWO THOUGHTS   by Walt Fluegel

Invisible in a place of my desire? A place of excitement, intrigue or maybe contentment? I have no such desire now. Honest. I don't want to be invisible. I no longer want to be secretive. I would like to be there in person, fully visible to everyone present. Maybe it's my imagination, or lack of it, that does not allow me to think of a situation. However, years and years ago in my early adolescence, ... well, you know the biology that happens during this time.

However, we are thinking of the present, not the past. I heard interviews on radio and television about the biologist J. Craig Venter who traveled all around the world to examine ocean water for microbial life. This biologist discovered numerous microbes new to our understanding of biomass and diversity. It gave us a different slant on what life, and new life he "invented" is capable of being. He did it through newer DNA technology. Would I have wanted to be invisible in his lab watching others do the work? Heck no!

I would have wanted to be there in person, getting my hands involved along with the rest of his crew. I would have wanted to ask questions, listened to discussions, examined some of the collected data, and watched events unfold. All that would have taken more than an hour because it takes many hours to find and evaluate discoveries. Discovery of new concepts, new insights, and new knowledge is a wonderful experience. I know, because I have discovered several bits of nature's knowledge on my own. Each thing I have found was a first time world event, and it was wonderful. And to share these discoveries with others worldwide is equally thrilling. Some of my discoveries are still being used as references to present work. It is a pleasant feeling.

Here is my second thought; I know I am invisible to you my readers, and you are invisible to me. How would I know of your presence? Where are you? I do not know how long it was before you opened this book and what article you read first or if my article is the last. I have made only part of

179

myself visible to you. On that same note we are all invisible to other writers throughout history. And in the present day of radio and TV, and various publications, we are all invisible to the producers of these products. But wait just a minute. They want to know who I am but in the meantime while I am invisible, I don't exist, and I do not make my presence known, unless I tweet immediately. When I watch TV for example I absorb. I contemplate. I am invisible as I analyze and enjoy the presentation for the most part. I sometimes grade programs as maybe a C or sometimes a B+, and on some occasions an A. The F programs are known almost immediately and surfed away.

As much as someone probing the deep heavens or the oceans to find what is out there, or numerous analysis, opinion polling, and other forms of surveys there are, all try to find out who or what is the invisible. Alternately, when it comes to me as an individual and part of the surveys I know I am not quite invisible, because I become part of a chart or just a dot or smear on someone's graph. My complete identity is still invisible. I do not mind being part of a graph, but I know the whole graph is not me.

My assignment hour of being invisible is almost over. TICK, TICk, TIck, tick, tic, ti, t, ...

> *When you help someone up a hill you are that much nearer the top yourself. (S. N. Kaatz)*

THE TALE IS REMOVABLE by Bob MacKean

His name was Mr. Grasser, probably not his real name, but it didn't take much to fool a bunch of money-hungry kids. We were all about twelve at the time just playing in the backyard of our house in Bloomington. A beautiful, new 1950 Oldsmobile kicks up dust as it climbs the hill coming towards us. It pulls over to the side of the road near our garage and a man climbs out. We gawk as he walks across the yard holding a briefcase. He seems nice but then asks a strange question. "Have we ever seen salamanders crawling across the road after a rain?" We tell him that we sure have. He goes into a story about how the University Of Minnesota Medical Center needs the salamanders for research. We are getting bored with the story until he gets to the part where he is willing to pay two cents for each one we can catch and save until he returns. Then he opens the trunk of the nice Olds to show us a wooden box filled with moss. He says it made to keep the salamanders healthy. We all agree to be collectors and can't wait until the next rain so we can make the big bucks. He tells us that the best place to find them, other than the road, is in the basement light wells around houses where they crawl in and can't get out—but—you must get there quick before they dig down.

The long-anticipated rain comes and four of us gather in the garage with buckets. It's still raining but we can't wait till it stops so we spread out all over the neighborhood looking for the black and yellow spotted toothless lizards. Sure enough, the critters are where he said they would be. We collect about three hundred and split up the six bucks we get when he comes the next day. He is so pleased that he raises the bounty to three cents for the next batch.

The next rain is very hard and we wait till it's over before we head out. The salamanders are plentiful but by the time we get to some of them, they have begun digging. We lose a lot of them because we can't pull them out of their holes without pulling their tails off. At three cents each we still make about eight bucks and are told that the next round-up will be worth five cents each. Now we're talking serious money

The next rain is warm and steady. The salamanders are coming out of the swamp behind our house and are everywhere. We pick up many as they try to cross the dirt road. The light wells have more than we have ever seen.

The buckets are getting heavy. Back at the garage we have a storage problem but we solve it by putting the cute little fellas in two big wash tubs that we found. We count almost five hundred and begin thinking about how we are going to spend our money

Mr. Grasser fails to come the next day and during the night the salamanders have climbed over each other and escape the tubs. My dad gets me up very early upset over what he found on the garage floor when he tried to get to his car. During the day we find a 55-gallon drum that holds our treasure and they can't crawl out.

Still, no Mr. Grasser. The barrel smells very bad and the contents are changing color, from black and yellow to grey. We're screwed, he's not coming and we have to get rid of a big smelly mess. We figure out how to get the barrel into a wagon and haul it down to the swamp. We know that the sick looking creatures will probably die and our humanitarian side urges us to help them to the other side. A quick trip to our homes to get our BB guns and we are back at the swamp to form a gauntlet that the beasts must penetrate in order to reach the freedom of the water. The barrel is overturned and they tumble down the hill. Many actually make it.

We never see Mr. Grasser again but learn later that a Chinese Restaurant in South Minneapolis has been closed down for using some strange meat in their chicken chow mien. I wonder what salamander tastes like. Maybe I already know.

MOTHERING THEN AND NOW by Pat Solomonson

Of all the Mother's Day cards I've ever received the one that stands out in my memory was the work of my son Mark at age 7. His second grade class assignment was to design a very personal Mother's Day message. His handmade card, carefully printed with red crayon on blue construction paper, read simply, "Mothers are the ones who are always right."

Now in his 40s, Mark has become very adept at tuning me out, albeit with a loving wink, every time I remind him about that.

It's hard to take ourselves too seriously after we've spent a good chunk of a lifetime in the mothering role. One of many incidents my family won't let me forget revolves around the "boot camp bran muffins".

It was that very emotional experience of sending a young son off to the military. We were gathered at the airport for our final goodbyes as Scott headed for Marine Corps boot camp. As I hugged him for the last time, I quietly tucked a package under his arm. It was a fresh supply, packed "to go," of his favorite bran muffins.

"I can just see him now," mused my husband after the departure, "face to face with his drill instructor, when he's questioned about what he's got in that package."

"Muffins, Sir, muffins from my mother," he would dutifully reply as my labor of love was confiscated.

Mother's Day always triggers a flood of memories for me. As a stay-at-home mom in the days when that was the norm, I thought I had the upper hand over those little rascals, most the time. I believe God gives every mother the required amount of psychic power to stay on top of things

Prophetic moms will always recognize reports of pain in a small belly as news that the teacher has scheduled a test that day. I recall the day I gave my fifth grader the benefit of the doubt. His teacher called to check. "Pain in the stomach?" she snorted. "If you ask me, I think it's a pain in his Social Studies".

Because the malady had run epidemic proportions that particular day, the teacher, one up on these connivers, rescheduled the test for a different date.

Maternal clairvoyance is even easier with very young kids. Like when your first grader swaggers home with a confident smile that means he's earned the respect of his peers. He plops his books on the table, faces you squarely, then announces in true 'big shot" fashion, "I told the teacher that you would......"

You know before he's even finished the sentence that he has volunteered your service to either (1) provide 32 popcorn balls for the Halloween party, (2) accompany the class on their field trip to a farm, or (3) provide summer vacation board and room for the white rat that now inhabits his classroom

While everyone knows that mothers hear all, see all and know all, there are times when we are caught off guard. We had a two-year-old acrobat who kept us all on our toes with his atrocious dinner table antics, all performed from varying positions in or on his high chair..

At one meal he suddenly stood up and fired a radish across the table, making a direct hit into his father's glass. He acted so quickly that none of us was aware of what was happening until we saw the splash of milk. This, of course, prompted much gleeful howling from all of his siblings.

Ah, the memories. I wish God's blessing on all the mothers who are still in the throes of raising children with the hope that you will treasure these years and not wish them away. You have the most important job in the world and you only get one shot at it.

Special tribute is due also to the many grandmothers who are now sacrificing much of their own personal time of life to provide the care needed, at least for a while, by grandchildren. I stand in awe.

The article below stems from conversations Max and I had often. She liked the article especially the very last. It is almost a quote from her.

NO GUNS by Walt Fluegel

Henrietta Parsons was deep in thought. Most likely she was thinking about what she and Rupert saw outside the store. ....And most likely it was intertwined with conversation they had often. ....Especially when they planned to go into town to deliver hay or buy necessities.

The wagon ride into town today was a bit bumpy. It rained heavily the night before and the horse seemed spooked as he misstepped on a loose rock in one of the ruts made deeper by the rain. On the way home, Rupert was humming a tune, but kept looking over at Henrietta.

"You haven't spoken a word since we loaded up in town. Cat got your tongue?"

"No Rupe. Just thinking."

"About what? Did we forget something from your list?"

"No Rupe, just thinking about that man. He was just lying there. Was he really dead? What about his family?"

"Oh! Come on Henrietta, you know he was dead. Some drifter I suppose. Didn't you see people coming to help him? Besides, I saw sheriff Jensen thrashing someone, ,,,,,,, probably the man who took the drifter out of this world."

"I still don't like it. Every time we go into town I hear about this man or that man being shot, some in arguments....some because of who knows why....they still get shot....and my lady friends tell me more....and my pupils tell of an uncle or big brother or cousin getting wounded in gun fights." She continued, "Why does everyone carry a gun when they are in town? You included. Can't you leave yours home?"

"Did you see a gun on that drifter? Did you see a gun belt?" Rupert asked Henrietta sternly. He did not let her finish but added, "If I carry a gun, others know! When others know, they leave us alone, and I don't pick a fight with anyone either." Henrietta did not respond. It was a slow quiet mile along the trail. The horse slowed to a walk. Rupert began to hum again.

They soon saw the schoolhouse where Henrietta taught general grades. In another month she would begin classes and wondered how many pupils there would be when school opened. Rupert broke the silence by questioning Henrietta, "Think you'll have enough to fill the grades this year?"

"Three less if the Kelleys leave. I hear Peter Kelley might have to abandon his farm. Peter has a hard time coping and with Irene being so ill all the time. They might go to her sister back East somewhere. Their three children will be a handful in any town bigger than ours."

Rupert added, "I don't think Peter really knows how to farm. Doesn't know animals." Rupert began to hum but stopped humming when he came into view of their farmstead not far from the schoolhouse. Henrietta was still in thought. "We got some mail in that box over there. Alan tucked it into the yardage of cloth at the last minute while you were talking to Mrs. Packer."

Mail was always delivered to the general store. However, the town council voted to establish a post office near the proposed railroad station if it ever came to town. That would not happen until the mine became more productive or the town grew.

Rupert and Henrietta always talked about the town's potential growth. Each understood the other's thoughts, but what could they, a farmer and a school teacher do about it? Rupert thought the mine would be the answer, followed by farmers coming to feed the miners and raising hay for the mules that hauled the rock and ore out of the shafts. Henrietta thought if the miners and some farmers could find wives to settle down with, the town would be more peaceful. A peaceful town grows. There would be fewer killings; there would be a general absence of guns around to do the killing. The women could help tame the men. Henrietta said this several times in the past year, either at home or while they were coming home from a hay delivery.

186

Each time she said the women would tame the men, Rupert slapped his hand on his revolver holster and said, "This tames men, not sweet talk from their women." He knew his wife didn't agree with him, but he sometimes added, "I have the gun handy just for show. If I don't start a fight, they know....they know, I have a good aim....if they start the fight."

This time Henrietta answered, "I feel safe with you even if you did not have your gun."

A GUESSING GAME AT THE GROCERY STORE   by Walt Fluegel

We were in the pasta section when someone behind us said loudly, "How are you today?" Was someone talking to us? We looked at each other and turned around to see the back of a woman who had just passed us in the aisle. We could not see who was being greeted. We both mouthed 'cell phone' as we noticed the familiar tilt of the head and the hand up to the woman's left ear. We did not see the phone except when we caught up or crisscrossed paths several times in different aisles. She must have had a good left arm because she was on the phone for the entire shopping trip.

Of course it was none of my business, but it was a bit of fun to speculate on what the phone conversation was all about. I decided to call the phone user 'Lily' since she vaguely reminded me of the ringy-dingy telephone operator played by Lily Tomlin.

I had no idea what the person on the other end of the line was saying. (End of the line? With a cell phone?) I made this overheard conversation into a game as my little gray cells conjured thoughts and speculated on who said what to whom.

"Oh that's great (chuckle). Why don't you tell Geri what you told me, ... she will love that one." Now who is Geri, I thought, and a she. My mind switched from Jerry a man's name to Geri when I heard the word 'she', a name for a woman I know could be Geraldine, spelled with a G. It must have been a joke because Lily chuckled again. All this time her right hand selected cans, boxes or bags as she filled her cart. At another time I heard

"....and tell Sam I'll see her next week when we ....". Sam...another 'her' - - I thought, must be Samantha. That's interesting. My thought was that maybe Lily could have hung up and called Sam herself, but then again Sam might not have a cell phone. Oh well, it's none of my business.

At one time Lily came into our aisle still chatting with her phone friend. This time she was clearly annoyed "...that Max is a real jerk, I should know." My mind switched to my Max (Maxine), and to have someone say Max is a jerk took me aback. And how did Lily know Max? "....yeah, I know, he's good to the kids, but he treats Bobbie like a maid." Bobbie must be his wife I thought but then Lily added, "...when we were kids he beat me and Francis lots of times until Frank took up wrestling. ...We're going to visit him this Sunday."

It intrigued me a bit to know that as soon as I heard the name Francis I thought of a girl name, but in Lily's conversation she either switched from Francis a girl to Frank or Frank was a boy sibling. I know it was none of my business and tried to dismiss such thoughts. I was impressed that, out of context, I could not discern whether the name was for a man or a woman until a gender was attached to it.

There was more chatting on the phone as we came close to checking out. Finally, Lily put the cell phone in her jacket pocket. In a moment another woman shopper came in the opposite direction and stopped her grocery cart next to Lily. Lily exclaimed in a joyful voice, "Jo is that *you*? Jo Anderson? When *did* you come into town?"

My gray cells began to work overtime! Jo? Joanne? Josephine?? A joyful answer came from Jo. "Toni where have you been all these years?" I did not have to guess who Toni was, Toni was Lily. I did not have to guess if Toni was a man or woman.

This ended the guessing game at the grocery store. But I did wonder later how many men or women names sound alike but are spelled differently.

GETTING CLOSE: OLYMPIC FACES   by Walt Fluegel

The camera was focused on the face of an Olympic coach. His head seemed firmly anchored, because it never moved. His eyes darted back and forth several times then dwelled upward on a distant scoreboard. A voice-over explained what had happened during the exercise while everyone was waiting for the scores. The voice continued and as the score was posted, the coach's mouth slowly pursed and his head made a slight left-right-left "no" motion. The voice-over was not needed. The coach's face said it all.

The summer Olympic events in London 2012 needed many skilled photographers to bring all different facets of the games to a worldwide audience. Other than watching teams compete, a viewer can see individual athlete's concentration and determination as cameras watch faces. For example when a gymnast makes a perfect dismount, his or her face tells whether the athletes believed they "nailed" the landing. If it wasn't perfect, we knew without being told.

What goes through the photographers mind while zooming on one unfortunate athlete? A fallen racer. We immediately see a closer look as the runner cups her hands over her face and we see her body shake as sobs overwhelm her, -- then in frustration she slaps the track several times. Similar disappointed tears occurred with male athletes too. What is going through the photographers mind? -- people in the control booth? --- and you? Is anyone heartless? Is it all in a day's work not to be affected?

The gymnastic sports are always reminiscent of a youth decades ago. Every high school gym had rings suspended from the ceiling. A skinny adolescent boy playing with those rings after school hours was a joy. But when the Olympic cameras showed the face of an athlete on the rings and making a cross with outstretched arms, that earlier joy changes to wonder. The camera first focused on the face as the athlete slowly went into the cross position. His face began to show more and more effort while he was maintaining this cross position. The lens slowly zoomed away so the viewer could see the massive shoulder and arm muscles vibrating as they did their work. Wonder and joy. It didn't matter to me if the athlete held his position for a required time or not. It was something very few other people in the viewing audience could master.

The face tell stories which we interpret in our own way. In an interval of a volley ball game the camera seemed to focus on one player bent over with her hands on her knees but looking through the net. The game was going badly for her team. They might lose. We slowly see the face come closer as the eyes look beyond the netting. The whole face and netting begins to fill the TV screen. Eyes are wide open. A voice-over tries to tell us what to think, but it is ignored. We have our own thoughts. In a moment later the TV screen switches to an overall scene of the game as a serve is to be made. Whether it was swimming or track and field, gymnastics, bike racing, or whatever the competition, there is always an end to the event and coaches and athletes look at scoreboards. Camera people scan just a few individuals so we see different facial emotions. In the instant the final scores are posted we know by expressions and subsequent joyful whoops who is the top scorer.

In any international competition most countries want to see their own "winners" so we see a waving of the "national flag" team in the stands expressing the joy when the winner is known. It can be from the final score on the field or on the scoreboard. National news also broadcasts an accumulating medal count and ranking. But we never see a count of joyful hugs or consolation hugs, or a count of the tears of pride or disappointment of athletes and coaches or friendly encounters between rival athletes. Sometimes the camera may come closer to individuals who hug their coach but notice it is not all smiles, perhaps an empty stare. But most of the coverage goes to the winning side's athletes, coaches, and fans. And soon after, there is an interview. You don't need to hear what is said, you just have to look at the faces. Are the almost-winners ignored? Sometimes.

The culmination of the Olympic event is the medal presentation often determined by a fraction of a second or points scored. The athletes have their medals and listen to their national anthem as the "gold" country's flag is raised. Each face tells its own story. A story of work, setbacks, challenges, time, persistence, refinements, and the final goal of an Olympic medal. As the anthem is being played some tears well up with national pride or self-fulfillment or final relief, while some join in mouthing the anthem's words. Sometimes there is a slight smile. What we see is a personal story. We have our own stories from distant comparisons as we continue to watch other events. Click, Walt

A BOY AND HIS DOG by Boyd Sutton

Consider this. You are six-years-old. You've just been torn away from friends—for the second time in as many years—by yet another move. You are living in a foreign country—Frankfurt, Germany—in the US Zone of Military Occupation just after World War II. The neighborhood you live in has no other American's with kids your age, and the Germans aren't friendly. Your dad is away most of the time. It's just you and your mom.

"I want a puppy!" More than the routine childhood desire for a pet, this was a plea for help.

Dad knew an Army general who had a springer spaniel with several puppies needing homes. One of the puppies—a bouncy female—selected me by coming over to chew on my shoelace as the other puppies remained huddled next to their mother. Frau Halder, the general's maid, told us that this puppy was the most active of the litter and was almost always off exploring somewhere. Whenever she'd go to check on the puppies, she would take count, come up one short, and say "nix da," which means "not there" in the dialect of German spoken around Frankfurt. So that's what we called our new puppy.

Nix Da was exceptionally intelligent and was the most loving dog I have ever known. Mom and I spent a lot of time with her and she learned quickly. She could do the usual roll over, sit up, play dead, and other tricks. But Nix Da would invent ways to take each trick a step further. You could ask her to sit up, then put a doggie bone on her nose and say, "Stay!" She'd remain in that position until you said, "OK." Then she'd flip her nose, sending the bone up in the air and catch it on the way down. She would stay in one place, even one position, almost forever if you asked her to. It saved her life one day.

I had taken Nix Da for a walk and she slipped her leash. She started to run across a busy road. There was a small median between the two lanes of traffic and when she got there I shouted for her to "Stay!" She stopped immediately and sat down. I waited for what seemed like an eternity for a break in the traffic, went out to the median, and put her leash back on. We waited for another eternity, then crossed back to the safety of the sidewalk. When we got home, I was so excited that I told Mom. I got in trouble for taking her out by the main road, and for crossing it myself. Nix Da was rewarded with a doggie bone. I didn't think that was fair, but it was OK because Nix Da was OK.

She was as much a playmate for me as a brother or sister would have been and was almost human in her actions. We had a small playground near our home in Frankfurt, and Nix Da would routinely accompany me as I went to play on the slide, monkey bars, or merry-go-round. She would climb up behind me on the slide's ladder, then sit and slide down like we kids did. She did it for pure fun, not just to follow me. Occasionally, when I played on something else, I'd look over and see Nix Da lining up with other kids to take her turn on the slide. Every time she came down, she'd run over to me, give me a lick and get a pat in return, then run back to take another turn on the slide. She loved that slide, and other kids would bring their parents to the playground just to see her do it.[1]

Nix Da was so gentle and sensitive that it was impossible to be angry with her, or even to be angry around her. When voices were raised in anger, Nix Da would come over and put her chin on your leg and look up with sorrowful eyes, as though pleading for you to stop arguing. If the argument persisted, she'd go whimpering from one person to another with that look in her eyes. She cut short many an argument.

We took her with us when Dad was transferred to England, but she had to remain in quarantine for six months due to England's determination to keep rabies off the island. We drove a half-hour each way to visit with her at least twice a week until she "got out of jail," as I called it.

Nix Da came along with us to Greece in 1951 (no quarantine this time) and quickly became a full-fledged member of the group of Greek kids I hung out with. She went everywhere with us. Occasionally, I'd forget that she was out with us when I went home and I'd close the metal gate to our yard with her still outside. There was no handle on the outside of the gate, but it had a small slit that I could reach my hand through to open the latch, which you had to pull sideways. Nix Da learned how to open the gate on

---

[1] The character of the neighborhood changed gradually as more Americans with children moved in and the Germans became more friendly. By the end of our first year in Frankfurt at least 10 – 15 kids routinely used the playground.

her own. I didn't train her; she just saw what I did and did it herself. Everyone talked about the dog that could open the gate. She never did learn to close it though.

Nix Da is the only dog I've ever known to understand commands in three different languages. When she did something wrong, we'd tell her, usually in English, "Go to your blanket." She'd drop her head and walk slowly to the blanket, curl up, and look at us with those sorrowful eyes. Sometimes, when we were living in Germany or Greece, we'd say it in those languages. Nix Da would head straight for the blanket. Friends would say, "She's only listening to your tone of voice," but we knew better. To prove it, we'd scratch her ears and play for a while. Then, we'd tell her (in German or Greek) to go to her blanket, using the same happy tone we used while playing with her. She'd trot off to her blanket, with her head up. She'd only put her head down when she knew we were unhappy with her. But she understood "Go to your blanket," (and other commands) in English, German, and Greek.

When we were sent to Iran in 1955, Dad decided Nix Da should remain back in the States due to the living conditions over there. So she went to live with my grandparents in Wickenburg, Arizona. We sure missed her, but when we saw the situation in Iran, we knew it had been the right choice. Dogs were not treated well there and diseases far outnumbered cures.

Nix Da quickly became Wickenburg' wonder dog. It's a small, sleepy town in the desert hills about 60 miles north of Phoenix—a lot like Andy Griffith's Mayberry, but with cactus and a lot hotter. Grandpa owned an air-conditioned pool hall and had a card table in the back. On a slow day— and most days were slow days—local businessmen came to play canasta, solo, cribbage, and other card games. My grandparents lived in an apartment upstairs.

When Grandpa wanted a beer, he'd tell Nix Da, "Go get me a beer." She'd take off upstairs, then he'd take a pool cue and bang on the ceiling. This was a signal for Grandma to get a bottle of beer out of the refrigerator, put it in a sack, and give it to Nix Da. "Take this to Jess," she'd say. Nix Da would run back downstairs with the bag held in her teeth, nose-open the pool hall's door, then run to the back and sit up on her hind haunches with that bag for Grandpa. He was so proud of Nix Da that he'd have her do it just to show off, even when he didn't actually want the beer. Just about everyone in Wickenburg knew Nix Da as the dog who fetched beer.

We were glad to get her back when we returned from Iran in 1959 and settled in Virginia. We thought she might not remember us after nearly four years, but she greeted us enthusiastically. When Nix Da wagged her stub of a tail, she wiggled her whole body. When she saw us this time she wiggled so much we were afraid she might hurt herself. We had our faces "washed" thoroughly and repeatedly by her licks. She slept on my bed that night and wouldn't take no for an answer, despite Mom's efforts—not mine—to get her to sleep on her own blanket. From then on she had bed privileges.

We enjoyed her company for three more years. As an only child, from the age of seven to 21 Nix Da had been my constant companion, my best friend, a substitute for the brother or sister I never had, only closer because she gave me all her love and devotion and we never argued.

I was away at college when she passed away. I was at a military school where I was surrounded by guys. I was 21, an adult, and I had a reputation to uphold. But I broke down and cried because Nix Da was then truly "not there."

UNCLE GUS' DOOR by Boyd Sutton

How can one door mean so much to a family? Well, knowing Uncle Gus and what he meant to our family, you might understand. Every family has an Uncle Gus. He isn't with us anymore, but his oddly-tilted door reminds us every day.

After I retired, Jean and I moved into the old family farmhouse where I grew up. Mom and Dad had passed on a few years earlier and, despite the distance from our home in the Cities, we had maintained the old place in good condition, often staying there on vacations, or going up for a traditional family Christmas. Even before Mom and Dad died, we had spent many a vacation with them in that house, and our two girls loved it there as much as Jean and I did. By the time we moved in, however, the girls were grown and married, with families of their own.

We knew we'd want to make changes to the house, but we decided to live there for several months before deciding on what to do, and in what order. Meanwhile, the girls and their families came up occasionally on vacations.

When they were growing up and we'd come to the house on family vacations, Mom and Dad slept in their bedroom on the main level while Jean and I slept in one of the three rooms on the second story. The girls shared another room, and a third was used as a storeroom. The one the girls slept in had an oddly tilted door. It looked as though the carpenter who had installed it was on a bender. It probably looked straight to him at the time.

In reality, my Uncle Gus, one of Mom's brothers, had built that door. He was handy with tools and loved to build things. But, as Dad liked to say— usually when out of Mom's earshot—Gus was always "a little off plumb." He meant that in more ways than one.

We all loved Uncle Gus. He always had time for us kids when I was growing up. In part that was because he never held onto a job for long. He wouldn't get fired. He'd just work until he had some extra cash, then he'd quit. Sometimes he'd say "Bye" one day and be gone the next on a trip— "gotta' go see the world," he'd say—then, just as suddenly, he'd appear on our doorstep with a hundred stories to tell. Often as not, he'd hitch a ride on whatever train happened by. Sometimes he'd thumb rides along the highway. I'm not sure he ever had particular destinations in mind, just a general direction—north, east, south, or west.

Mom used to say he'd probably get killed by some "pervert" or fall off a train drunk and get run over by a hundred boxcars. She loved him too, but she didn't like what she called his irresponsible ways. "And, stop puttin' crazy ideas into the kids heads with your stories," she'd say. But she'd listen to them just as raptly as we did.

During the Great Depression, jobs were awfully hard to come by and Gus couldn't make enough money to rent a room anywhere around the home place, so Mom and Dad agreed to let him stay in their home and help on the farm. The upstairs had only two rooms then—Jillian's and mine. Mine was nearly twice as big, so they decided to build another room by dividing mine in half. Uncle Gus did the carpentry.

First, he built a stud-wall to divide the room. Then he had to knock down a part of the hallway wall to create an opening for a door to the new room. He framed it in nicely, but the left side was about three-quarters of an inch higher than the right side. No one noticed it until it came time to put the door on the hinges. Then you could see the gap at the top left.

I remember Dad and Gus arguing whether the frame was off plumb. Dad insisted it was and Gus insisted it wasn't. Gus settled the matter by getting out his plumb bob and stringing it from the top frame on each side. "By golly," Dad said, "it sure as shootin' is plumb, all right."

The trim around the doorframe was already on and Gus didn't want to take it off and rebuild the entire frame, so he took the door apart instead and rebuilt it so the left side was three-quarters of an inch higher than the right side. Then there were no gaps, top or bottom, and the door swung nicely. But that combination of doorframe and door, both three-quarters of an inch higher on the left side, made it look oddly tilted.

Gus lived with us off and on for about four years, interspersed with his occasional trips—here today, gone tomorrow, back in anywhere from two weeks to a few months, always with great stories to tell—until the Japanese bombed Pearl Harbor. Gus signed up for the Army the next day.

He might have gotten a farmhand deferment, as so many others did around here. But Gus said, "Nope! I gotta' go fight the Japs, 'n besides, I gotta' go see the world." That's the last we ever saw of him. He survived Saipan and Tarawa, but was killed on Iwo Jima. We must have received a hundred letters from him, all with upbeat stories about the "great" places he was seeing, places that I later learned were jungle hell-holes of dirty hand-to-hand fighting with the Japanese. But that was Gus, always upbeat. He never met a half-empty glass in his life.

Eventually, Jean and I decided to remodel the three small upstairs bedrooms into two equally large rooms, more appropriate as guest quarters when both of our daughters and their families visited. But we decided that we'd keep Uncle Gus' oddly tilted door. After all, that door is family.

BEFORE YOU SAY CHEESE by Walt Fluegel

A group of writers and a photographer were discussing that writers and photographers have their own way of describing a scene or painting or capturing a scenic picture. The discussion swirled around whether a picture is worth a thousand words or if any picture can tell a story without any explanation. Or must some explanation be given to the picture. Then one member of the group, Mary Jacobsen, told a story of her great grandparents in a family photo. I will include her remarks at the end of this article but it sparked an idea and a question. My thought ran something like this; if there is a group photo, what is the reason for that gathering? Can the photo tell us any reason? Must there be an explanation not known from the photo?

Many group photos requires folks to bunch up or make a line or form some closeness before a photographer gives the signal "Now say cheese!" before he trips the shutter. Once the photo is processed and distributed, each person in the photo has his or her own recollection of the event. So right off the bat there is an explanation that must be given. And for very old family photos, the stories of the gathering are passed on to generations down the line. So what are the stories?

Suppose we do not know what the story is? When we as strangers are given a group photo for the first time can we find a story for ourselves in the photo?   We ask, what are the stories in a family gathering or gathering of politicians, group photo of teacher and students, club outing, and other gatherings? Among politicians it might be easy enough to deduce the story if there are several other well-known people in the frame. But what about that one person in the photo no one recognizes yet is in a prominent position next to a popular senator for example? What was that story? Who can tell it?

But suppose too, in an old family photo one person has not said "cheese" on command by the photographer? In fact, that one face seems to be dower, apprehensive, and not like the other joyous images of that same person in the family album. Was it just one bad moment?

With this last question let me insert Mary's involvement of the discussion. It is part of a short story she had written some time earlier describing getting ready for an 1895 group photo involving her great grandparents. The story starts with the kids getting ready for the photographer to arrive. I take it from there „,

Whenever I look at the photograph of my mother's family (my mother is the baby) I always imagine such a scene occurring just before the photographer arrives.

In the photograph, my grandmother, looking serene but serious, sits queen-like next to her husband, my stern-faced grandfather who is holding, but otherwise ignoring, the baby on his lap. The baby, sober faced as well, with big round eyes, is wearing a white lace bonnet and a long, white pleated dress. The other children stand in a row with frozen faces, the girls looking pained in their tightly sashed, white dresses, and the boys in white shirts and black trousers, seemingly wanting to grin but not daring. Most people in photographs of that era were posed like that.

There is no way of telling what really happened before the photographer squeezed the bulb. I had no way of knowing, until my Aunt Ann told me, that my grandmother had been terrified that my grandfather, dead drunk, would drop the baby.

A photograph does not always tell the whole story. A picture is not always worth a thousand words.

May I add my comment: ..... but some of those words are saved and passed to the next generations.

MY IDEA OF LOVE Boyd Sutton

Linguists debate whether or not the Inuit language has five, 50, 150, or more words for "snow." But there is no disagreement that "there are huge numbers of basic, unrelated terms for huge numbers of finely differentiated snow types," as one scholarly study notes. The same is true for ice. That's because snow and ice play such a large role in the Inuit's lives, even to the point that their lives depend on precise terminology. When you consider how important love is in our lives, it's a wonder that we don't have more words in the English language to differentiate different types of love.

We distinguish among different forms of love by adding adjectives—puppy love, romantic love, filial love, marital love, one-off "love" (an artful term used in England and Australia equivalent to what we would call a one-night stand). Even these additions, however, don't capture the essence of love in its many permutations. Instead, we need lots of words to get to the heart of the matter (and I hope you enjoy that thoroughly intended pun).

The word "love" is full of meaning and, perhaps more than any other positive word, subject to misinterpretation. If, for example, I were to come up close to my friend, Mary, and say quietly, "I love you," she would raise her eyebrows and probably take a step back. Her defenses would go on high alert. Her mind would race. She would think, "What does he mean?" If any of you overheard it, you would think, "Oh oh," and then be off to the races with other thoughts, from the curious to the salacious. But I would merely be expressing the love I have for a friend. We do love our friends, don't we? And I know that after Mary thought about it, she'd accept that happily.

Now, if I were to come up to my friend, Bill, and say, "I love you," reactions would take another direction. Bill wouldn't just take a step back, he take a step way back—way, way back. And the rest of you would immediately have a different view of me.

If in a moment of maudlin madness I simply said to the entire assembled group of people in the room, "I love you people," your reaction would be entirely different. Some would say, "Aw, isn't that nice." Others would have different reactions. But no one would likely think ill of me.

All of this is to illustrate a simple point. "Love," means so many different things to so many different people in so many different contexts that it's a shame we don't have more words for love. On the other hand, maybe it's a good thing that there is only one word, because the basic meaning is the same in every context. Love just is. It means that I feel a connection with a person, that they mean something special to me, that I would "do for" her or him.

When you think of it, "do for" is the key. It transcends all forms of love, from the love of a father or mother for their children, husband and wife for each other, friends, even lovers. It's also true of the altruist's love of humanity. He wants to do things for people, things that make their lives better. God's love is a "do for" love as well. After all, he gave his only Son for us that we might be saved. That's a really big "do for."

People often confuse the wanting of each other that strongly characterizes romantic love—that physical attraction one sees portrayed in the movies, on television, and in books—as true love. It isn't! Certainly "wanting" is involved in romantic love. But love means wanting to "do for" someone (or others) so badly that you ache inside. You want to give her a home, security, happiness, and safety. You want to take away her pain when she hurts. You want to sustain her joy when she's happy. You would go to any lengths to "do for" the ones you love. If all a person wants is to get something, it's not love. Love is not selfish. True love is wanting to "do for."

BEN'S BOUQUET by Jennifer Tahtinen

Ben passed over only a few weeks ago. We'll miss him. Odd how, within a short sweep of the clock's hand a life becomes no life. And not one thing can be done about it.

Once Ben told me that, as a child, he'd had no parents; an aunt raised him, he said. I thought perhaps that was why he navigated the years calm and cooperative and sort of unnecessarily yielding. All that early emotional pain, at some point, was neatly folded, tied with strong ropes, and contained by an obedient disposition. Ben, the boy with warm brown eyes and a good amount of unruly brown hair immersed himself in learning and the rewards that come with being an outstanding student. Alone in the large world Ben applied caution in his dealings with others. After all, an aunt raised him, he said. She could never be a mother and, surely, an aunt was no father!

Continuing into college even when it was nearly impossible to pay one's own way, Ben found education — and a woman! A strong, intelligent young woman, who also had determination and was making her own way, too. Neither had any easy backing for their efforts -- no parents' money underwrote them! Advancing by one's own means and effort is never easy and, generally, no one appreciates the supreme efforts required when one cuts his own path step by step.

Fortunately, Jane was the right woman for Ben. They laughed together, they used their exceptional minds to challenge one another, and they loved one another. They loved within a deep, secure channel that many never realize can even exist.

When Ben enlisted in the Air Force, he had no choice but to leave his young wife at home. During World War II, though, many young wives were "here" while their husbands were far away "over there." Only a few wives, however, received the telegram Jane did: "This is to inform you that your husband Ben was shot down. Believe he is prisoner in Germany. Status unclear. Update to follow." Perhaps the emotional strength Ben had practiced while a boy was of great value to him... he, unlike others, stayed alive. There were days and months of unspeakable, ugly, tortuous treatment. It was the Russians that, after fifteen long months, at last freed Ben and the others.

When all that became part of his past, Ben and Jane resumed life together. Soon they bought a home, had good jobs, and had two children - a girl and then a boy. There were lingering medical issues from Ben's wartime imprisonment. His stomach, for one thing, continued to give ongoing problems. He never revealed to me exactly all the repercussions of those years but there was a variety.

Ben advanced at work. He became head of his department. He was known for being kind, conscientious, industrious, and accurate. It was no surprise that his children achieved well. Certainly this gave him and Jane—a huge measure of joy.

During the last years Ben endured quite a lot of pain. Jane had died suddenly from a heart attack four years earlier. For a time Ben managed; he still volunteered at the living history museum, he still kept in touch with old friends from the square-dance club, he still was active in his faith, he still read and wrote, and lovingly gazed at pictures of his four fine grandchildren.

One day driving home from his volunteer stint at the museum, he sort of fell asleep and inadvertently drove into a concrete pillar. The car was totally wrecked. Ben, somehow, was not hurt. The children immediately got his driver's license cancelled, and they signed up an in-home health care agency to care for him. Over a year slid by as medical appointments, prescriptions, and overnight care became Ben's final chapters. Then, that one morning, Ben left us; it seemed abrupt and unexpected. But his suffering had become constant and we wouldn't have wanted him to continue.

I told the florist "it must be an exceptionally lovely bouquet," adding that the flowers be regal purple with a background comprised of glossy greens. Somewhat reluctant, I agreed to the suggestion that a variety of purple tones might be effective in making a statement of loveliness. Then I further directed that the vase must be clear, transparent glass--nothing milky, translucent or opaque. In my mind only the sparkle of clear glass would be a proper choice for Ben!

Leaving the florist shop and driving home through the winter snowfall, I felt sad that it wouldn't be possible for me to travel across the country to be there for the burial; I wouldn't be there to place a shovelful of dirt on my dear friend's grave. Some comfort came to me knowing that I had done my very best to send the loveliest bouquet I could manage. Flashing into my mind came the poignant thought about the ribbon!

The momentary turbulence about the ribbon was quieted by a realization. Whatever ribbon adorned the bouquet, Ben would think it very fine; yes, he would be pleased and find any bouquet whatsoever with any ribbon whatsoever to be very fine, indeed.

> *Don't tell me the moon is shining; show me the glint of light on broken glass. Anton Chekhov*
>
> *If it is worth writing at all it is worth writing well.*

AT THE WEDDING by Doris Hanson

Three Little Flower Girls, all dressed alike,
Waiting their turn down the aisle to take a hike

Baskets of rose petals they carry with pride
To create a pretty path on which to usher the bride.

The first little flower girl came slowly down the aisle
Then spotted her mom and made a quick exit, to be at her arm.

The second little flower girl went on to the front
And set herself down on the platform kerplunk!

She looked in her basket and to her surprise,
There in the bottom more petals she spied

So quickly overturned her basket with glee
And petals all over the floor we could see.

At the front of the church stood the pastor so stately and tall,
With a look on his face that made us wonder in awe

What does he see that makes his face quiver.
That strange look, is making me shiver.

I whisper to Mary Ann, 'What's going on?"
"I don't know," came her reply!

For us to look behind, we didn't think proper,
But why is the pastor looking so awkward?

Finally the ring bearer, a handsome young lad
Wearing white shirt and tie, with a vest of soft green,

black shoes and trousers, sees someone he knows
Then leaves the aisle to be by his dad

The third little flower girl was not yet on her way,
Oh my goodness, I wonder what is the delay

Is she crying, is she sick, is she hurt, is she shy?
There is definitely something that has gone awry

What seemed like forever, to us seated in front?
We felt helpless and nervous beyond expectation

Whatever it is I hope it's not serious or bad
This is a celebration, not a time to be sad

At last the Maid of Honor appeared.
With a smile on her face that reached ear to ear.

She was holding the hand, of the flower girl so fair
Who had thought it her job to pick up the petals lying there.

She had sat on the carpet without any worry
And picked petals one by one, no need to hurry

Into her basket she gently placed them.
Isn't that sweet what her thoughts had been?

Now the father proceeded with the bride by his side
He was strong, yet letting go wasn't easy

The bride smiled and kissed him. Then turned to her groom,
And the Wedding proceeded as Love filled the room.

MAKING A NEW FRIEND by Bob MacKean

My boss said, "Here, you get to read the copy for Bernice's column." As the rookie proofreader at the Leader newspaper, I felt lucky to have the job and did whatever I was told. I asked who Bernice was as I compared her hand-written story to the printed copy that would appear in the paper. I missed a few corrections that should have been made because the column was so humorous and interesting I didn't even look at the spelling and punctuation. I learned my lesson and was careful not to get too engrossed in the copy I read. I was introduced to Bernice one day as she came by the proofreading office on the way to the archive room to research her column. We became friends, and she made a point of stopping by my desk each week to chat for a while.

Years later, I decided to join the Northwest Regional Writers Club and there she was to welcome me. Each month she would have a fascinating story to read and with her eyesight beginning to fail, she would often ask if I would read her assignment. My own story would usually pale to her beautifully crafted tales.

I have lost a friend and mentor for now but look forward to seeing her smiling and radiant face in God's Kingdom someday.

VALENTINE by Stan Miller

I looked in the dictionary for meanings of words I thought I knew. And to my surprise, each and every word was given the same meaning, and I'll mention a few.

Modest, fair, enthusiastic, knowledgeable, friendly, encouraging, and then I stopped for now. Who would have guessed these different words had the very same meanings somehow.

I pondered that thought at length, thinking I had been looking amiss. The more I thought, the more I believed Old Webster was wrong, on this.

I was stumped, as a fallen tree might say, and I didn't know what to do. Then I asked a friend about my dilemma, this friend oft tried and true.

"Well," he said, "It won't matter if you choose other descriptive words, for there are many more. I'm sure as I was born, the answer will be the same as before."

I wanted to argue, of course, and ask, "How could this be?" But I thought better of that, as another thought came to me.

Computers are just the thing, I thought, for on the Internet, much knowledge is sought. So I sought out another friend, one who could help this computer search begin.

She typed in a thing or two, the machine whined and then a fuse blew. I was ready to call it a day, when the computer lit up the display. And there to my wondering eyes should appear, one phrase we now, commonly hear.

Now, the words she had previously entered, were in alphabetical order and perfectly centered. Down at the bottom, in capitals, of course, were the same definitions I found at the previous source. They were one and the same as the dictionary had said, and my pulse quickened and raced in my head.

Yes, all of the words had meanings the same and my list, so much longer became. Then I was in for another surprise, for the phrase, "made a difference," leapt to my eyes.

"Of course," I muttered when I settled down. I was no longer stumped like the tree that was down.

This story, amazing but true, included a scavenger hunt too. Now I don't recall each and every clue, but the one I remember, I'll read for you.

All of these words, one lady defines

She made a difference, in your life and mine

Writers club charter member, we toast

The answer is found behind the sign post.

Of course she was all these attributes and more and she made a difference, that is for sure.

THE SWEDISH PSYCHE by Pat Solomonson

Swedes are by nature very patient, polite and long suffering. I know, because I am married to one.

We were part of a large contingent of Swedish choruses attending an international convention of Swedish singers in the Twin Cities.
The visiting Swedes were a friendly bunch. Their fun- loving personalities were never more evident than when they would spontaneously burst into song, whenever and wherever they felt moved to do so.

We were housed at a large hotel in Bloomington for the convention, but the final Grand Concert was held on the Bethel College campus in Roseville.

Chartered buses took everyone from the hotel to the concert hall. Most of the chorus members were transported on an earlier bus, meaning I would be traveling alone. I chose the bench seat in the rear.

From that vantage point I watched as Swedish singers and their spouses fiddled with those little knobs above the seats that are supposed to control the air conditioning.

The women singers were appropriately costumed in long skirts, long sleeved blouses, and colorful red flowered shawls over their shoulders. The men were in their chorus uniform suits. Not the kind of attire anyone would choose for a sultry summer night.

Discomfort was apparent throughout the bus. I wondered how long it would be before one of those perspiring, heavily clothed Swedes would rise up, approach the driver and complain about the air conditioning!

As the only non-Swede passenger on that fateful journey, I noticed that Swedes also share a common type of stress response. More specifically, it's a lack of any noticeable response to stress.

Women were now shedding their shawls and rummaging through their purses for a piece of paper, anything with which to fan the face. Men were removing their jackets. The heat was stifling. Perspiring brows were mopped.

Faces took on worried looks as fumes gradually filled the overheated bus. Had they suffered enough? Would someone say something? Would no one complain?

Finally! A woman seated near the front made her way up to the driver. Soon she turned back, shrugging her shoulders, indicating she got no explanation from the driver. Not only did the driver fail to speak or understand Swedish, he was also unable (or unwilling) to communicate at all.

Then it happened. The bus sputtered and died right there in the middle lane of the busy highway leading to the college. People started toward the door.

Swedish reserve had a bit of an edge now as passengers raised their voices, ever so slightly, to tell the driver, "We've got to get out of here...will you please open the door?" The driver, pointing to the traffic light, indicated that we would get out, in small groups, each time the light changed to red, so we could safely make it across the busy highway.

The wait seemed forever. Coughing and wheezing were the only sounds now, though I suspect some choice words were being uttered, ever so quietly... and in Swedish, no doubt... so as not to offend the driver.

Finally, the short-on-words driver finished shepherding his flock of disgruntled passengers across the highway, where we all waited (patiently, of course) for some word about Plan B.

It was beginning to resemble the Immigrant Trail.....right out there on the shoulder of that busy highway. The colorful little band of stranded Swedish singers, steadying themselves in the rough turf, prompted curious stares from three lanes of traffic whizzing by.

Turning their faces away from dust, churned up by passing cars, most of the Swedes were still smiling, some even joking about their predicament. Those with cameras took advantage of the situation to capture their travel companions posing as hitchhikers.

Suddenly, like a mirage, a rescue bus appeared. The driver proved to be sufficiently verbal, even jovial, and the bus was cool and free of fumes.

When I met up with my husband after the concert, he wanted to know how it went, meaning my bus trip over to the concert hall. I told him it was an interesting study of the Swedish psyche.

"It made me realize, dear, that you're not so odd after all."

"Tack så mycket" was his polite reply.

> *I have never found in anything outside of the four walls of my study an enjoyment of equal to sitting at my writing desk with a clean page, a new theme, and a mind awake. Washington Irving 1783 - 1859*
>
> *Finding the stories is not the hard part. Writing them down is.*
>
> *Proulx*

A PLACE APART by Arlu Ames

My place apart is five feet above the ground. It's moveable and muscular. On sunny days the heat rises from a silky coat to leave a tangy, musky scent in the air. I can feel the horse's movement up my spine to the base of my neck. Not a jarring or unpleasant sensation, just the careful placement of each hoof sending liquid pulses through my frame. I'm connected to the horse-muscle to muscle, nerve to nerve, emotion to emotion.

When I ride, I am for a short time, removed from the stressors of life. Perhaps it's because horseback riding is such an overwhelmingly sensory experience. There are the sounds of creaking leather and the muffled thud of hoof steps. My vision takes on a different perspective as I am lifted up high. My balance is challenged and enhanced by the gentle rocking motion beneath me. And let's not forget the occasional contest of will that takes all my focus to problem solve.

Why do I feel better after time spent on the back of a horse? The factual explanation is that, during riding, the movement of the horse causes the right and left sides of the brain to communicate with each other. "Feel good" chemicals called endorphins are released producing a natural high as powerful as prescription narcotics.

There is a reduction in stress while blood pressure and pulse rate are lowered. This translates into an intuitive perception of wholeness and contentment.

An awareness of well-being and serenity overtakes me when I ride. Circumstances seem to lose their magnitude and become more manageable. Only my perspective has changed, but what a difference that makes. For a short time life is not as overwhelming, my teenagers all get along, financial stress is relieved and my husband is even better looking!

Separated from time and problems, horseback riding is a serious vacation from reality. Just for an hour, just for a while, a place apart.

A PLACE APART by Walter Fluegel

After a long walk, I had come up to the driveway when I heard , "Look Mom, look what I just caught!" I turned toward the voice of my landlord's kid and I heard her say "Where did you get that jar? Didn't I tell you not to use any of my jars for your ...." She didn't finish because she saw me and stopped in mid scold. At that moment, I felt sorry for that kid as I looked at the jar with a butterfly fluttering inside. I was just a new renter, in a new town, and I felt helpless in the situation.

At that time, I was a new microbiology grad student, unattached, young, and eager to get my degree. But that scene haunted me for a long time in a strange way. I thought that if I ever had kids of my own, I would not do that to any of them. Let them have all the jars they wanted to capture any and all critters.

Of course that was some time ago and you might ask if such a thing ever happened to me. Did anyone squelch my collecting. Strangely no. But then again, in the orphanage there was no opportunity for anyone to make any collection of anything except stamps. Our housemother neither encouraged nor discouraged anything, but she did run a tight ship. But strangely again, the orphanage was a place where I slowly became aware of a vague thought, a cloudy thought that solidified sometime after I was completely on my own, making a living for myself and family. I found pleasure in the things I did, not in the place I did them. It still happens to me.

Many people find pleasure, or comfort, or refuge or renewal in specific places, a place apart from the daily routine of living or working. We can think of going fishing to let the river wash away the troubles of the day even though the freezer is full of fish. Or painting mountain or seaside scenes again and again, after a season of city business.

Maybe going on retreat to hear speakers extoll a different way of thinking. Or even going to Disneyland or Branson. Anyone of the many places apart from daily chores seem the natural thing to do for scores of people.

I know it happens in thousands of different ways. But Walt, what about you?

It is not a place, but what happened that seems most important to me. And if I were to narrow it down a bit it was discovering newness for me, discovery of a world I had not seen before, discovery of my own potential, discovery of my limits, discovery of how others see the world they live in, and most of all, discovery of the natural world, of living things. This narrows down to a strong interest in biology. As you might guess, biology is not a place, not a thing but a concept.

When I was finally on my own as a biologist and exploring the natural world, one discovery tops all discoveries because it was the first of many as a biologist, yet it is not unique to me. It is universal. It is very human. Let me explain.

It should not matter to the reader what kind of biology I was exploring but to understand the end result. I had seen something others saw many times. In fact they did everything they could to control the observation, or prevent it from happening. It interfered with a mindset that everything should be as it always was with other microorganisms. But I reasoned that nature provided the bacterium I was investigating this certain property of adhesion or clumping or growing on the container walls rather than growing dispersed as "all the other bacteria" known. In short, I took advantage of the adhesive properties and to make a long story short, I managed to do research on answering questions others were asking about this particular group of bacteria. I tried to understand nature, not to bend it to preconceived thought. I gave public talks of my work and publish several research papers on the topic. Review articles still site my work.

It was not my first time discovery of something new in the biology world that is my place apart. But the feeling of accomplishment when discoveries happen again and again, not only to me but to others. I am no longer in the position of doing biological research, but I read from time to time of other biologists and other researchers in the many fields of discovery whether it be in astronomy, anthropology, paleontology, or other disciplines. I can "feel" their joy of discovery, the answering of questions they have asked of nature.
Breaking down the barriers of orthodox thinking. I seem to "relive" the same path they took because I know the feeling each researcher must have for being the first one to have made that one discovery. It is a very good feeling.

215

I hope for the youngster who found the butterfly that it was not the place he found it, or the jar he was not supposed to take, but the joy of finding the critter in the first place. It would or could be a discovery of many more to come if he were not discouraged by a scolding. The pleasure of discovery is a place apart but universal throughout life for most of us.

A PLACE APART by Don Miller

Cherryvale Park had proudly manicured green lawns. People would gather, time to time, friends, family, out in the sun or even inclement weather. On occasion, there was even singing—of Negro spirituals, blues, or folk music. There were marble and granite statuary and multicolored flowers in a variety of kinds. It was a place of solitude, broken only by the whispering wind or song of birds. It was surrounded by a wrought iron fence, there only to keep out vandals who sought to deface the park's contents.

Outside it from time to time a parade would appear, led by a black, extended length, station wagon. It would park outside the entrance gates that held aloft the sign—CHERRYVALE PARK OF ETERNAL REST— sole cemetery in Atherton, Wisconsin, Hickerson County.

ALMOST ON EMPTY by Alice Ford

Almost on empty is bad enough, but running on empty is the pits and I have been there more than once. This man I married use to like to fill up the gas tank and then run it on empty before adding more gas. How many times I prayed for God to keep us going, and you know he always did. I can't say we ever really ran out of gas.

Let me tell you about one time in upper Michigan and we were nearly out of gas. It didn't matter we drove right past the gas station. He would get it in the next town. When you go to the lake shore there is usually a hill going down into the city. Thank You God that is just what we had as we crested the hill above the town, the engine stopped. Friend husband put the truck in neutral and we coasted all the way down the hill and into a gas station.

This happened to us more than once. One time we were going into Downing and ran out before we got over the hill, You know that car went over the hill and down the street and didn't stop until we were right in front of the gas pump. I'm not sure if he's just lucky or if he has his own guardian angel.

Even our granddaughter learned his habit and sometimes as we are getting into the car she   would say, "Grandpa, are you sure we have enough gas?" She was about six when she first noticed his gas was on empty, now she is 23 and she still 'checks his gas tank.

One time in Texas, the gas was low but he decided the gas was too high and he was going to go to the next state. May I repeat we are in Texas. Did we make it. we must have, I don't remember sitting along the road side.

On the toll road the gas stations are usually about 30 miles apart. l can tell you that this is just how long we can even after the empty bell goes off Thirty miles I recall one time driving through Mississippi we drove right past a gas station, and he noticed the gas was a penny cheaper. You know we turned that R.V. around and went back. Not sure we saved a penny.

Now I'm not sure what things have changed. We don't dare let the gas get down under half full. I'm happier and I think the angel has pushed that car long enough, and now it's high time for common sense to take over. The high cost of gas this summer helped keep the tank full as it just cost too much to let it get empty or maybe he heard it was hard on the alternator.

However Half empty is no longer a word at our house.

DESTINY IN TIME by Walt Fluegel

Write about a different time you might have liked to have lived in.

Let's start with the concept that what people do in time results in history. The assignment presumes that the writer knows history well enough to make comparisons of places, dates, events, personalities, culture, geography, seasons, climate, technology, politics, religions, and human nature. All these things plus many more become jumbled with time never to be repeated exactly. However, each segment of time may be unique, but very very familiar.

Let me try to explain. Knowledge tells us that humans seem to be an endless repeating pattern of behaviors. Humans have always shown love and hate, compassion and indifference, jealousy, envy, pride, sadness, joy, and many other labels we attach to different facets of what it is to be called human.

The expression "history repeats itself" or "if you do not learn from the past you may repeat it" seems associated with wars or hard times of a country or era. A current example is the observation that worldwide, the rich are getting richer and the middle class is dwindling. This is a recurrent theme going back to Stone Age times. The consequences are "good times" for a few and less than that for the many. Someone comes along and tells the masses that they have an answer to the problems, but you must follow me for your salvation. The solution can be wars, political action, upheaval, change in religion, a new way of life, government, or rarely a peaceful transition. New leaders arise while some fall, with maybe enlightenment or stagnation or a new kind of oppression. So it matters not what era in history is chosen there is no place I would want to go back to but remain right where I am. Because I think history does repeat itself, I know this present time best of all. It spans the best of times to the worst of times and a lot of middle ups and downs.

In my lifetime I have known of several wars, peaceful times, advancements in civilization, science, medicine, man on the moon and machine explorers on Mars, marvelous and numerous inventions and technology, political assassinations, oppressive and benevolent governments, social experimentation, disparity in income or education and many other opposites. But it all boils down to me, the individual. What did my time do to me -- or what did I do in my 84 year time?

One of my college mates in Alaska had an expression "geography is destiny." Here is an example. My mother, a recent widow emigrated to America with me as a baby and brought us to America in 1929. If I remained in Germany, I probably would not be alive today to tell you about times flow. The Hitler Nazi times were harsh on people who were or became deformed. I developed a back problem. Or I might have been killed by Allied bombs during WW2 because my parents lived in a highly industrial area.

My life in an orphanage in Mt Vernon NY until I was 14 was considered the usual thing and average for that time and there is a long story about that. I must have learned some survival mechanisms. At the orphanage I developed a love of learning, always liked school, and finally became an academic in biology in my late 20's. Knowing biology helps me understand the human organism. I say helps, ... not know, ... the human organism.

I have had my 'glory days' in college as a student in Alaska and a mix of other glory days and disappointments several times through academia. I failed to get the PhD degree twice. Getting a PhD was supposed to train a student to do research, but I did research on my own and know I have contributed to science in several ways and higher education in a small way. I have several science publications but, if I were truly a writer there would have been other writings I could point to as part of that success. On a day to day basis I was only an average in convincing colleagues to see things my way. Socially, I was hardly on the radar screen having my wife Maxine being the strength in this category. I also had 'glory days' in publishing photo information in a national magazine and as a member of camera clubs.

As a biologist, I can say that with a reasonably happy marriage for 54 years until death did us part, we managed to have produced our replacements; a boy and a girl. Both were a joy. But a disappointment; their marriages did not last. Reasons can only be told by them, I can, but will not speculate why.

219

Some folks say that I have an imagination, but I cannot imagine a time from the past that has had as interesting a background for me to have survived this long. I am sure there are or were others "out there" who have lived through the same gamut of things I listed for myself above. Their geography was or is different from mine. But I also know that in a strange way, destiny is shaped by being one complex human organism called Walt Fluegel.

The Girl with the Pearl Earring by Johannes Vermeer 1665

THE GIRL WITH THE PEARL EARRING by Denis Simonsen

Often called the Mona Lisa of the North or the Dutch Mona Lisa this painting by Johannes Vermeer is not dated but thought to have been painted in 1665,. Today it is kept in the Mauritshuis Museum in The Hague.

As an image it was chosen to be recreated in words for a monthly writing assignment. It is interesting to note that even though the subject is a familiar one, the name and the story behind the model were uncertain. With this in mind each writer constructed a story and the results revealed a great deal of diversity in depicting the uncertain history.

Read and enjoy our creativity and come to your own conclusions knowing that quite possibly you or any one of these writers may be closer to the truth than might be imagined.

PEARL VISION by Stan Miller

As she sat for the portrait
Her earring caught my eye.
I asked how she came by it
She paused before her reply.

Her Father loved the ocean
Was a diver so I'm told
Spent time in exotic places
In search of Pirates gold.

No one knows for certain
Just what happened then
And no one ever found out
He was never seen again!

His gear was found days later
On the bottom near the great reef,
And a purple drawstring pouch
Tied in a banana leaf.

They brought all to our home
The banana leaf uncurled
Inside two nuggets of gold
And this priceless pearl

Now as I tell this story
It still gives me release
In due time it brought comfort
And gave me a little peace.

I'm told an ocean creature
When disturbed by a sand grain
Will secrete a substance
To alleviate the pain.

In due time that irritation
 Becomes a lovely pearl
An object to be fashioned
Into jewelry for a special girl.

So in the hands of a master
That irritating thing
Becomes a piece of beauty
Like a necklace or earring.

Though I wear it in mem'ry
 Of a dad I barely knew
It reminds me to be patient
And I pass that on to you

I've learned a great lesson
 From this creature of the sea
As irritants of this life
Come to vex and annoy me.

This pearl helps me recall
That irritations are not new
They have pestered all mankind
But there's help to guide me through

I secrete a little prayer
Around that pesky grain of sand
And it becomes a thing of beauty
When placed in the masters hand.

THE GIRL WITH THE PEARL by Alice Ford

This must be the coming out party for this beautiful fourteen year old girl. Her name is Jewel and she is the daughter of an Eastern Mediterranean Monarch. We notice not a scrap of hair is showing. She probably was bathed, perfume and dressed by others. The earrings were a present from her father. They are awfully heavy but she won't say a word.

Despite all the finery she doesn't seem to be very happy about being there. She is questioning an overheard conversation on her left. She also has a secret that she is not sharing with anybody. I can sense the fear in her eyes as she is watching the parade of old men who are there to look he over. She doesn't seem to have a very strong back and her shoulder s almost sag in that dress, yet jewel has strong facial features she will grow into.

Will one of these men take her away from everything she knows? Jewel has come to a crossroad in her life and she cannot walk away from it. She knows that if the man who takes her is not happy with her, her own father will have to kill her. Is there any escape for her? No matter where she goes she will be followed and taken back.

She has made plans in her short span of life and has a secret she does not share with anyone except a missionary friend she happened to meet while buying a scarf for her hair. There is an underground community that will get people out of the country and into safe havens. She has to leave this very day while the men get together for drinks and conversation. Jewel will take a walk in the garden where one of the gardeners has permission to take one of the trucks in for an oil change. He too will be gone and the truck will be found in a drainage ditch.

THE REAL STORY By Don Miller

The young woman, Katrin, had been approached by the sculptor , DeGausse about posing nude for his latest sculpture. She was told that she would be admirably paid. DeGausse was known for sculpting statues of great attraction. The studio was bleak, dark and cold, matching the overcast day outside. As per instructions, Katrin arrived at 9:30 a.m. De Gausse placed in her hand her payment, a large pearl earring, motioned distractedly at a wooden screen in the corner of the room and told her to disrobe. Her clothing fell to the floor, all she wore was a woman's Turkish turban and a single pearl earring .and the intense cold worked it's magic until the tips of her breasts were hard and cold as ice.

DeGausse's sculpture was to be called "the Virgin." He was working the clay with his fingers to build a prototype he could use to make the actual sculpture. He soon cursed the inadequacy of his small spirit stove, the clay had stiffened to the hardness of his models nipples.

 "Well, with this cold it's just no good, Katrin, there's a painter named Vermeer that should be here in an hour, you've been paid already and might as well pose for him , go behind the screen and put on one of my dirty brown jackets and get warm."

DEAR BABBY by Mary Jacobsen

Assignment "Don't trust that guy"

.

I am a 12-year-old girl who everyone says is mature for my age. Except my alleged parents who treat me like a nut case. My problem is this: I can't get ready to leave the house without my father shouting, "Don't you dare step out that door, Young Lady! I won't have a daughter of mine looking like a tart." I swear the whole block can hear him.

He's 32 and thinks we're still living in the dark ages. Anyway, he's old. Nobody says "tart" anymore. When he says he's just thinking of my health I give him my "look" (I'm good at sarcasm). He says that anyone who leaves such large swatches (his word) of skin exposed to the elements is courting, most certainly, fatal pneumonia. It's embarrassment, though, I'll most likely die from, if any of my friends hear him. To embarrass me even more, he calls my low-riders, "hip huggers."

My father is the nut case, if you ask me. And my mother's just as bad except she uses shorter words.
My boyfriend, "Todd," (not his real name) agrees that my father is nuts and wants me to leave home and go away with him. What do you think, Babby? Should I go with "Todd"?
Girl with nutty father

Dear Girl with nutty father:

If you are as mature as you seem to think, you would try to be more understanding of your parents' position and not use terms like "nut case." They love you and want only the best for you. You might explain, calmly and reasonably, what fashion means to you. If you find it difficult to get through to your parents, particularly your father, you may consider obtaining the services of a family therapist. However, you should realize that shouting under such circumstances is normal in a man your father's age.

As for your boyfriend, "Todd," my advice is, don't trust that guy.

FRIDAY, THE THIRTEENTH by Don S. Miller

Trish Anderson and Davis Forbish were young lovers—who spent six passionate years living together—and finally had scheduled their marriage on Tuesday, February 18, 2009. Davis—known to speed a little too much—had a whole slew of tickets he kept tacked to the walls of his den with pushpins.

They awakened on the morning of Friday, the thirteenth, to a breakfast of steaming hot black coffee, croissants with butter, and strawberries with melted chocolate. They had breakfast at 8:00 am and they were on the road at 9:30 am, busily talking about where they were going to spend their honeymoon.

On the morning of Tuesday the 18th, they were arrayed in their best: he in a tuxedo he'd bought in the men's clothing store: *Maurice's*, in Montevideo. Six of his best friends, including the best man: Peter Tyler, also in tuxes, were there to support him. She, in her bridal gown, makeup brought a wonderfully healthy glow to her skin. Her father and brothers, all in tuxes were there to support her and all her bridesmaids were fitted out in their wedding day dresses. Momma, Poppa, her brothers and all the members of the wedding party were in tears as is common on these occasions. Friends and family came from all across country.

Side by side they spent several hours in the church, the front of the church was alight with candle flame and the scent of flowers wafted through the air. Thoughts of those in attendance were: *They look so good together, she so beautiful, he so handsome. This is their special day.* Some remembered them, *as they were as children, at play in the yard, the first time they rode bicycles alone, how excited she'd been after her first kiss that she had to tell everyone about it.*

Finally, Pastor Cecil Lazarus said, "Open your hymnals to the Service for Burial on page one-hundred forty-seven…"

FRIDAY THE 13TH by Boyd Sutton

Friday the 13th? It's a great day. While others cower, I celebrate my great good fortune that I was raised to ignore superstition, to laugh in its face, to poke it in the eye. My trips always begin on Fridays. My dinner parties always have an even dozen guests so that, with me, the number comes to 13. I gleefully alter my course to walk under ladders. I'll cross a busy street when I spot a black cat, just so it will cross my path. When it rains, I try out all 13 of my umbrellas, opening each one indoors until I know I have the right one for that particular rain. I set the salt shaker on the edge of the table where it's likely to get knocked to the floor, spilling its contents. I adore flagstone walkways, stepping on every crack I can find. I even looked in on my wife as she dressed for our wedding. Well, that one was a mistake. I've been stuck with her for 40 years. At least she's willing to review everything I write.

Please send flowers to Room 220, St. Croix Falls Hospital. They say I'll be out of traction is a couple of weeks.

DON S MILLER (1963 - ?)

Born at the beginning of the psychedelic sixties and its love generation, although a bit too young to take a shot at free love myself. Child of the apathetic seventies, and the golden age of rock you could actually understand—singer-wise. Absent Without Leave and left in total mental amnesia through the uneventful eighties. Present in body only wasting away in a factory through the latter half of the nineties. Anyone else remember the Y2K hoax? The New Millennium, became a Borg, Borg assimilator implanted 9-13-2001. Joined the real writing world, found my niche in dark fiction, very dark sometimes, will turn 50 in 2013, and life has been a happy happy gumdrops carnival ride.

DENIS SIMONSEN

Denis grew up near Grantsburg WI, attended a one room country school and graduated from Grantsburg High School. Encouragement by his parents to become an avid reader at an early age fostered his love for books and an appreciation for both prose and poetry He has always enjoyed creative writing but after retiring he expanded his horizons by joining other writers and sharing his sense of creativity.

Poetry is his passion but he enjoys occasionally composing a short story or recalling on paper, events that have occurred in his past. Whatever he writes he tends to emphasize feelings and emotions that go along with experiences and places. He hopes these contributions to this book project those feelings. Denis lives near Siren WI, with his wife Liz. He has two grown children and two grandchildren

TINA WIDELL

Tina is a CNA at the Grantsburg nursing home and mother to 5 boys. She started writing for a creative writing class in the fifth grade and it has been a passion ever since. She won the auxiliary's patriotic essay contest in the eighth grade. She now uses her writing for self-expression, difficult communication, and as a hobby. Writing is engrained in every part of her mental and physical being. Though she loves her current job, she deems writing as the only thing worth doing.

RUSS HANSON

Russ retired after a career as a teacher and then a scientific computer programmer, began writing for his own pleasure, soon making it a hobby, then adding a weekly newspaper column, followed by a blog, Facebooking, thus turning the hobby into an obsession. He has it under control with regular attendance at a writer's group where each member begins by saying "My name is Russ. I am a writer. I have been writing daily for 792 days now…."

Russ has self-published a seemingly endless series of local history and local nostalgia books, some which have sold as many as 300 copies. You can find his writing and photos at riverroadrambler.blogspot.com where nearly 25 folks read every word of his blog.

He is the treasurer of the Northwest Regional Writers club and never fails to have the bank balance up-to-date. He will tell you that he is one of the most modest, humble and unassuming people in all of the Midwest, and possibly North America. His photo here was a self-portrait taken live into a mirror. The fuzzy focus captures his essence.

WALT FLUEGEL

Walt is a retired biology professor from the University of Minnesota at Duluth, and now resides on Johnson Road a mile or so west of Grantsburg. At UMD he taught microbiology and other biology courses and did research which produced several published papers.

His hobby in Duluth was photography which led to two in depth How-To articles in a national photo magazine. He continues his photo hobby here in Grantsburg and added monthly articles to his hobby time for camera club newsletters. A sample of these articles can be found in this book.

His other writing experiences range from being a reporter for college papers, and an occasional writer for a community newspaper in the Twin Cities (Northeaster) and of course this club.

Walt's motto is -- Have Fun.

BOB MACKEAN

Bob was born in Minneapolis in 1937 and grew up in the Seven Corners neighborhood near where the new 35W bridge is now. He went to nearby Vocational High School where he expected to learn the printing trade. He joined the Navy after graduation and worked in his uncles' radiator shop for five years after he was discharged. In 1965 he started working at Rosemount Engineering becoming an aerospace assembly manager.

Webster, WI, became his home in 1979 when he went to work for McNally Industries. In 1991 he went to work for the new St. Croix Casino in Turtle Lake. In 2001, at age 64, he retired and became a long-arm machine quilter with his wife, Betty. Their business , Christmas Valley Quilting, is still going strong.

His writing career began after he worked at the Inter County leader for a time as a proofreader shortly after Bernice left an empty desk. He joined the Northwest Regional Writers club in 2004 and with the support of his family, the legend continues.

STAN MILLER

Stan grew up in Falun WI. and graduated from Grantsburg High School
He played football at Macalester then Bethel college.

Upon graduating he taught history at Luck High School for 34 years and
coached football wrestling and track.

In 1962 he married Jackie Wirth of Siren and together they raised four
children: Kathy, Alicia, Kini and Eric. Nine grandchildren have become
part of the family.

In 1995 Riley, a granddaughter, died of sudden infant death syndrome. Her
death was the catalyst for a plethora of poems

Besides writing for Northwest Regional Writers he contributes to his
church's newsletter monthly.

Second place was given to Stan's poem "Ben Gay and a prayer" at the
Writers conference in Spooner WI. in 2011. A children's book "The Night
before Easter" is scheduled to be published late in 2012.

ALICE FORD

I, Alicemaree Ward, grew up in the back rooms of a hard ware store in Downing, WI. I finished her last two years of High School at Glenwood City, WI. I then took a short secretarial course in Eau Claire taking a job with Ed Phillips and Sons in Eau Claire until I married Charles Ford in 1947.

Charles was a farmer and I was not a complete city girl as I had spent five years during the depression on a farm. Even with all that, both of us were young and had a lot to learn. The third year, Charles developed something called Undulant Fever and at that time there was not a cure. He was told if he wanted to stay alive he would have to leave the cows behind.

Our world was recovering from the war and unemployment was very high. Nevertheless, Charles always had a job. None of them were easy, and it required moving often. In 1955 he was hired at a dairy in Beloit, WI., and was able to later transfer to Menomonie, WI. (HOME at last). A good man we knew sold us a house where we lived for 35 years and raised our five children, retiring in1987.

Most of our lives we raised children and paid the bills saving a little for retirement. This has provided great memories and you will find laughter, joy and tears in my writings.

MARY JACOBSEN

Soon after moving to northern Wisconsin in 1992 Mary joined the Northwest Regional Writers. She's a member of Yarnspinners, a local critique group, and the Wisconsin Writers Association.

Mary writes fiction and non-fiction often based on experiences and people from her Chicago and Wisconsin childhood. Much of her writing reflects the 30 years she and her husband, Ed, spent outside of the United States living in Turkey, Spain, Kenya, Swaziland, and France. Her published work includes play reviews and several award winning stories and articles.

KATHY KRANZ

Into each life some hardships must come. Kathy has had her share of trials and heartaches.

She has schizophrenia,, She touches on this subject in a book she wrote. It wasn't until Kathy met Gene that she found the love and acceptance that she had searched for all her life. After being married to Gene for one year she was termed as a "stable schizophrenic." This is the best you can get with this disease, Kathy says.

Gene and Kathy shared a ministry together. No, they were not professional singers, but God used their mistakes and touched people's hearts anyway. They did not preach a theology, but rather they pointed people to Jesus. If God would never have loved, Jesus would never have died.

Theirs was a whirlwind courtship, whirlwind marriage and a whirlwind death. Gene and Kathy's courtship lasted three months before he asked for her hand in marriage. They were engaged one year and their marriage lasted seven years. Gene was killed in a car accident on November 7, 1999.

Who says love only comes in fairy tales? Her book deals with Kathy's experiences after Gene's death, and how Kathy leaned on God and depended on her faith to get her through the hardship of losing her beloved husband.

BOYD SUTTON

Boyd was born in Arizona, raised in Europe and the Middle East in a foreign service family, and spent 37 years in varying assignments in the US Army, Central Intelligence Agency, and National Reconnaissance Office. He is now retired and lives with his wife, Carmen (Hable), on her family's farm near Siren, Wisconsin. They have two lovely, married daughters and three granddaughters, with twin grandsons in the hopper. Two horses, two dogs, and a cat pretty much control their lives.

After writing professionally for most of his career, and being unable to publish due to the nature of his work, Boyd is living his dream of writing for fun—and, perhaps, a little profit. He enjoys reading—and writing—humor, essays, poetry, and, especially, fictional thrillers. He has been published in several magazines and newspapers. His first novel is in the works. Boyd produced and edited *The Wisconsin Writers' Journal* from 2005 through 2009, then became Executive Director of Wisconsin Writers Association in 2010 – 2011.

Boyd has won numerous writing awards, including a Jade Ring (top prize in the WWA), 1st Place in the Florence Lindemann Humor Writing Contest, and multiple 2nd, 3rd, and Honorable Mentions. He was awarded the first Fidelia Van Antwerp Award for Exceptional Service by the WWA in 2012.

PAT SOLOMONSON

Pat Solomonson's interest in writing began as a child when she collected pen-pals. She edited her high school newspaper, then majored in journalism at Macalester College. She worked part time at various Twin City newspapers while raising five children. She is a past president of Northwest Wisconsin Regional Writers.

Pat was widowed a age 39 when her first husband was killed in a firefighting accident. She later met and married Rudy Solomonson, who has roots in Polk County, Wisconsin. They now live on Dunham Lake in a home that was formerly her lake cabin.

In 1970 Pat's life took on a whole new focus when her eldest son was diagnosed with a serious mental illness. Appalled by a lack of appropriate treatment, support services and community understanding of mental illness, Pat became a tireless advocate and educator. She founded the Mental Health Advocates Coalition of Minnesota, now a part of the National Alliance for the Mentally Ill and has been the recipient of numerous awards and recognition for her efforts.

Made in the USA
Charleston, SC
25 November 2012